Rick Steves®

SNAPSHOT

Stockholm

CONTENTS

INTRODUCTION

This Snapshot guide, excerpted from my guidebook *Rick Steves Scandinavia,* introduces you to Stockholm, the bustling capital of Sweden. With its modern buildings and dedication to green living, Stockholm has the feel of a gleaming metropolis, but it offers a satisfying blend of Old World charm and 21st-century tech. Start at its core with a stroll through the Old Town, Gamla Stan. Then visit the *Vasa* Museum with its 17th-century warship, the Nordic Museum covering five centuries of Swedish lifestyles, and Europe's original—and unsurpassed—open-air folk museum, Skansen. Indulge yourself in this city's aristocratic delights, including the Changing of the Guard at the Royal Palace and the elaborate *smörgåsbord* at the Grand Hotel. For a side-trip, visit Drottningholm Palace, the royal family's opulent summer get-away, or Uppsala, a classic university town with a soaring cathedral. Then catch a boat and unwind among Sweden's rocky garden of more than 30,000 islands—Stockholm's Archipelago. Here in Stockholm's playground, you can count the pretty red cottages, go for a lazy stroll or bike ride, or relax on a sandy beach.

To help you have the best trip possible, I've included the following topics in this book:

• **Planning Your Time,** with advice on how to make the most of your limited time

• **Orientation,** including tourist information (abbreviated as TI), tips on public transportation, local tour options, and helpful hints

• **Sights** with ratings:

    ▲▲▲—Don't miss

    ▲▲—Try hard to see

    ▲—Worthwhile if you can make it

    No rating—Worth knowing about

- **Sleeping** and **Eating,** with good-value recommendations in every price range
- **Connections,** with tips on trains, buses, boats, and driving

Practicalities, near the end of this book, has information on money, staying connected, hotel reservations, transportation, and more.

To travel smartly, read this little book in its entirety before you go. It's my hope that this guide will make your trip more meaningful and rewarding. Traveling like a temporary local, you'll get the absolute most out of every mile, minute, and dollar.

Ha en bra resa! Happy travels!

Rick Steves

SWEDEN

SWEDEN

Sverige

Scandinavia's heartland, Sweden is far bigger than Denmark and far flatter than Norway. This family-friendly land is home to Ikea, Volvo, ABBA, and long summer vacations at red-painted, white-trimmed summer cottages. Its capital, Stockholm, is Scandinavia's grandest city.

While it's still the capital of blond, Sweden is now also home to a growing immigrant population. Sweden is committed to its peoples' safety and security, and proud of its success in creating a society with one of the lowest poverty rates in the world. Yet Sweden has thrown in its lot with the European Union, and locals debate whether to open their economy even further.

Until 1996, Swedes automatically became members of the Lutheran Church at birth if one parent was Lutheran, and up until the year 2000, Sweden was a Lutheran state, with the Church of Sweden as its official religion. That's now changed: Swedes can choose to join (or not join) the church, and although the culture is nominally Lutheran, few people attend services regularly. While church is handy for Christmas, Easter, marriages, and burials, most Swedes are more likely to find religion in nature, hiking in the vast forests or fishing in one of the thousands of lakes or rivers.

Sweden is almost 80 percent wilderness, and modern legislation incorporates an ancient right of public access called *allemansrätten*, which guarantees the right for anyone to move freely through Sweden's natural scenery without asking landowners for permission, as long as they behave responsibly. In summer, Swedes take advantage of the long days and warm evenings for festivals such as Midsummer (in late June) and crayfish parties *(kräftskiva)* in August and September. Many Swedes have a summer cottage—or know someone

who does—where they spend countless hours swimming, soaking up the sun, and devouring boxes of juicy strawberries.

While Denmark and Norway look westward to Britain and the Atlantic, Sweden has always faced east, across the Baltic Sea. As Vikings, Norwegians went west to Iceland, Greenland, and America; Danes headed south to England, France, and the Mediterranean; and Swedes went east into Russia. (The word "Russia" has Viking roots.) In the early Middle Ages, Swedes founded the Russian cities of Nizhny Novgorod and Kiev, and even served as royal guards in Constantinople (modern-day Istanbul). During the later Middle Ages, German settlers and traders strongly influenced Sweden's culture and language. By the 17th century, Sweden was a major European power, with one of the largest naval fleets in Europe and an empire extending around the Baltic, including Finland, Estonia, Latvia, and parts of Poland, Russia, and Germany. But by the early 19th century, Sweden's war-weary empire had shrunk. The country's current borders date from 1809.

During a massive wave of emigration from the 1860s to World

Sweden Almanac

Official Name: Konungariket Sverige—the Kingdom of Sweden— or simply Sweden

Population: Sweden's 9.9 million people (about 57 per square mile) are mostly ethnically Swedish. Foreign-born and first-generation immigrants account for about 17 percent of the population and are primarily from Finland, Poland, and the Middle East. Sweden is also home to about 20,000 indigenous Sami people. Swedish is the dominant language, with most speaking English as well. While immigrants bring various religions with them, ethnic Swedes who go to church tend to be Lutheran. For background on everything in Swedish society from religion to the Sami people, see www.sweden.se.

Latitude and Longitude: 62°N and 15°E, similar latitude to Canada's Northwest Territories.

Area: 174,000 square miles (a little bigger than California).

Geography: A chain of mountains divides Sweden from Norway on the Scandinavian Peninsula. Sweden's mostly forested landscape is flanked to the east by the Baltic Sea, which contributes to the temperate climate. Sweden also encompasses several islands, of which Gotland and Öland are the largest.

Biggest City: Sweden's capital city, Stockholm, has a population of 897,000, with more than two million in the metropolitan area. Göteborg (526,000) and Malmö (307,000) are the next-largest cities.

Economy: Sweden has a $498 billion gross domestic product and a per capita GDP of $49,800—similar to Switzerland's. Manufacturing, telecommunications, automobiles, and processed foods rank among its top industries, along with timber, hydropower, and

War II, about a quarter of Sweden's people left for the Promised Land—America. Many emigrants were farmers from the southern region of Småland. The House of Emigrants museum in Växjö tells their story (see the Southeast Sweden chapter), as do the movies *The Emigrants* and *The New Land*, based on the books of Vilhelm Moberg.

The 20th century was good to Sweden. While other European countries were embroiled in two world wars, neutral Sweden grew stronger, finding equilibrium between the extremes of communism and the free market. In the postwar years, Sweden adopted its famous "middle way," an economic model that balanced the needs of the democratic state and the private business sector.

The Swedish model worked very well for a while, providing a booming economy and robust social services for all. But the flip side of those ambitious programs is one of the highest tax levels in the world. After a recession hit in the early 1990s, some started to iron ore. The Swedish economy is one of the strongest in Europe, helped by its competitive high-tech businesses—and by the government's generally conservative fiscal policies. Some 71 percent of Swedish workers belong to a labor union.

Currency: 8 Swedish kronor (SEK) = about $1.

Government: King Carl XVI Gustav is the ceremonial head of Sweden's constitutional monarchy. Elected every four years, the 349-member Swedish Parliament (Riksdag) is currently led by Prime Minister Stefan Löfven of the Social Democratic Party (elected in October 2014). *The Economist* magazine—which considered factors such as participation, impact of people on their government, and transparency— ranks Sweden by far the world's most democratic country (followed by the other Scandinavian countries and the Netherlands, with North Korea coming in last).

Flag: The Swedish flag is blue with a yellow Scandinavian cross. The colors are derived from the Swedish coat of arms, with yellow symbolizing the generosity of the people and blue representing vigilance, truth, loyalty, perseverance, and justice.

The Average Swede: He or she is 41 years old, has 1.88 children, and will live to be 82.

criticize the middle way as unworkable. But Sweden's economy improved in the late 1990s and early 2000s, buoyed by a strong lineup of successful multinational companies. Volvo (now Chinese-owed but Sweden-based), Scania (trucks and machinery), Ikea, H&M (clothing), and Ericsson (the telecommunications giant) led the way in manufacturing, design, and technology.

The global economic downturn of 2008-2009 had its impact on Sweden's export-driven economy: Unemployment ticked upward (although it remains enviably low compared to other countries), its famously generous welfare systems felt the pressure, and its Saab car manufacturer filed for bankruptcy protection. But Sweden has rebounded since the crisis, and the country's fortunes have outpaced those of the European Union—Sweden's main export market.

Historically Sweden has had an open-door policy when it comes to accepting immigrants (the country's immigration laws are the most generous in Europe). Since the 1960s, Sweden (like Denmark and Norway) has accepted many im-migrants and refugees from south-eastern Europe, the Middle East, and elsewhere. This praiseworthy hu-manitarian policy has dramatically—and sometimes painfully—diversi-

fied a formerly homogenous country. Many of the service-industry workers you will meet have come to Sweden from elsewhere.

More recently, with refugees flooding in from Syria and Iraq, Swedish social services have been tested as never before. The pol-itics of immigration have become more complex and intense, as Swedes debate the costs (real and societal) of maintaining a culture that wants to be blind to class differences and ethnic divisions.

Though most Swedes speak English, and communication is rarely an issue, a few Swedish words are helpful and appreciated. "Hello" is *"Hej"* (hey) and "Good-bye" is *"Hej då"* (hey doh). "Thank you" is *"Tack"* (tack), which can also double for "please." For a longer list of Swedish survival phrases, see the following page.

Swedish Survival Phrases

Swedish pronunciation (especially the vowel sounds) can be tricky for Americans to say, and there's quite a bit of variation across the country; listen closely to locals and imitate, or ask for help. The most difficult Swedish sound is *sj,* which sounds roughly like a guttural "*h*w" (made in your throat); however, like many sounds, this is pronounced differently in various regions—for example, Stockholmers might say it more like "shw."

English	Swedish	Pronunciation
Hello. (formal)	*Goddag!*	goh-**dah**
Hi. / Bye. (informal)	*Hej. / Hej då.*	hey / hey doh
Do you speak English?	*Talar du engelska?*	**tah**-lar doo **eng**-ehl-skah
Yes. / No.	*Ja. / Nej.*	yaw / nay
Please.	*Snälla. / Tack.**	**snehl**-lah / tack
Thank you (very much).	*Tack (så mycket).*	tack (soh **mee**-keh)
You're welcome.	*Ingen orsak.*	**eeng**-ehn **oor**-sahk
Can I help you?	*Kan jag hjälpa dig?*	kahn yaw **jehl**-pah day
Excuse me.	*Ursäkta.*	**oor**-sehk-tah
(Very) good.	*(Mycket) bra.*	(**mee**-keh) brah
Goodbye.	*Adjö.*	ah-**yew**
zero / one / two	*noll / en / två*	nohl / ehn / tvoh
three / four	*tre / fyra*	treh / **fee**-rah
five / six	*fem / sex*	fehm / sehks
seven / eight	*sju / åtta*	*h*woo / **oh**-tah
nine / ten	*nio / tio*	**nee**-oh / **tee**-oh
hundred	*hundra*	**hoon**-drah
thousand	*tusen*	**too**-sehn
How much?	*Hur mycket?*	hewr **mee**-keh
local currency: (Swedish) kronor	*(Svenska) kronor*	(svehn-**skeh**) **kroh**-nor
Where is...?	*Var finns...?*	var feens
...the toilet	*...toaletten*	toh-ah-**leh**-tehn
men	*man*	mahn
women	*kvinna*	**kvee**-nah
water / coffee	*vatten / kaffe*	**vah**-tehn / **kah**-feh
beer / wine	*öl / vin*	url / veen
Cheers!	*Skål!*	skohl
The bill, please.	*Kan jag få notan, tack.*	kahn yaw foh **noh**-tahn tack

*Swedish has various ways to say "please," depending on the context. The simplest is *snälla,* but Swedes sometimes use the word *tack* (thank you) the way we use "please."

STOCKHOLM

If I had to call one European city home, it might be Stockholm. One-third water, one-third parks, one-third city, on the sea, surrounded by woods, bubbling with energy and history, Sweden's stunning capital is green, clean, and underrated.

The city is built on a string of islands connected by bridges. Its location midway along the Baltic Sea, behind the natural fortification of its archipelago, made it a fine port, vital to the economy and security of the Swedish peninsula. In the 1500s, Stockholm became a political center when Gustav Vasa established the monarchy (1523). A century later, the expansionist King Gustavus Adolphus made it an influential European capital. The Industrial Revolution brought factories and a flood of farmers from the countryside. In the 20th century, the fuming smokestacks were replaced with steel-and-glass Modernist buildings housing high-tech workers and an expanding service sector.

Today, with more than two million people in the greater metropolitan area (one in five Swedes), Stockholm is Sweden's largest city, as well as its cultural, educational, and media center. It's also the country's most ethnically diverse city. Despite its size, Stockholm is committed to limiting its environmental footprint. Development is strictly monitored, and cars must pay a toll to enter the city. If there's a downside to Stockholm, it's that the city feels wealthy (even its Mac-toting hipsters), sometimes snobby, and a bit sure of itself. Stockholm rivals Oslo in expense, and beats it in pretense.

For the visitor, Stockholm offers both old and new. Crawl through Europe's best-preserved old warship and relax on a scenic harbor boat tour. Browse the cobbles and antique shops of the lantern-lit Old Town. Take a trip back in time at Skansen, Europe's first and best open-air folk museum. Marvel at Stockholm's glittering City Hall, slick shopping malls, and art museums. (Even "also ran" museums in this city rank high on the European scale.) Explore the funky vibrancy of the design-forward Södermalm district.

While progressive and sleek, Stockholm respects its heritage. In summer, military bands parade daily through the heart of town

to the Royal Palace, announcing the Changing of the Guard and turning even the most dignified tourist into a scampering kid.

With extra time, consider one or more Stockholm side-trips, including the nearby royal residence, Drottningholm Palace; the cute town of Sigtuna; or the university town of Uppsala, with its grand cathedral, Linnaeus Garden and Museum, and Iron Age mounds (see the Near Stockholm chapter). Stockholm is also an ideal home base for cruising to island destinations in the city's archipelago (see Stockholm's Archipelago chapter).

PLANNING YOUR TIME

On a two- to three-week trip through Scandinavia, Stockholm is worth at least two days. For the busiest and best two- to three-day plan, I'd suggest this:

Day 1

10:00	See the *Vasa* warship (movie and tour).
12:00	Tour the Skansen open-air museum and grab lunch there.
14:30	Walk or ride tram #7 to the Swedish History Museum.
16:30	Ride tram #7 to Nybroplan and follow my self-guided walk through the modern city from Kungsträdgården.
18:00	Dinner at one of my recommended waterfront restaurants, or take a harbor dinner cruise.

Day 2

10:00	Ride one of the city orientation bus tours (either the hop-on, hop-off or the 1.25-hour bus tour from the Royal Opera House), or take the City Hall tour and climb its tower.
12:15	Catch the Changing of the Guard at the palace (13:15 on Sun).
13:00	Lunch on Stortorget.

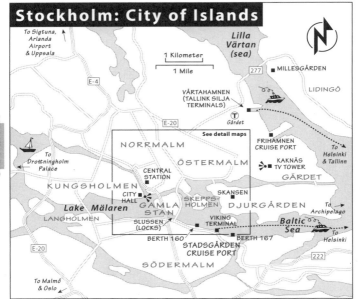

14:00 Tour the Royal Armory (if it's reopened from its renovation; if time and budget allow, also consider the Nobel Museum and/or Royal Palace sights), and follow my Old Town self-guided walk.

18:30 Explore Södermalm for dinner—it's just across the locks from Gamla Stan—or take the Royal Canal boat tour (confirm last sailing time).

Day 3

With an extra day, add a cruise through the scenic island archipelago (easy to do from Stockholm), visit the royal palace at Drottningholm, take a side-trip to charming Sigtuna or Uppsala (see next two chapters), or spend more time in Stockholm (there's plenty left to do and experience).

Orientation to Stockholm

Greater Stockholm's two million residents live on 14 islands woven together by 54 bridges. Visitors need only concern themselves with these districts, most of which are islands:

Norrmalm is downtown, with hotels and shopping areas, and the combined train and bus station. **Östermalm,** to the east, is more residential.

Kungsholmen, the mostly suburban island across from Norrmalm, is home to City Hall and inviting lakefront eateries.

Gamla Stan is the Old Town island of winding, lantern-lit streets, antique shops, and classy cafés clustered around the Royal Palace. The adjacent **Riddarholmen** is similarly atmospheric, but much sleepier. The locks between Lake Mälaren (to the west) and the Baltic Sea (to the east) are at a junction called **Slussen,** just south of Gamla Stan on the way to Södermalm.

Skeppsholmen is the small, central, traffic-free park/island with the Museum of Modern Art and two fine youth hostels.

Djurgården is the park-island—Stockholm's wonderful green playground, with many of the city's top sights (bike rentals just over bridge as you enter island).

Södermalm, just south of the other districts, is sometimes called "Stockholm's Brooklyn"—it's young and creative. Apart from fine views and some good eateries, this residential island may be of less interest to those on a quick visit.

TOURIST INFORMATION

Stockholm's helpful city-run TI—called **Visit Stockholm**—has two branches. The main office is downtown in the Kulturhuset, facing Sergels Torg (Mon-Fri 9:00-19:00—until 18:00 off-season, Sat until 16:00, Sun 10:00-16:00, Sergels Torg 3, T-bana: T-Centralen, tel. 08/5082-8508, www.visitstockholm.com). There's also a branch at the airport, in Terminal 5, where most international flights arrive (long hours daily, tel. 08/797-6000).

Around town, you'll also see the green *i* logo of **Stockholm Info,** run by a for-profit agency. While less helpful than the official TI, they hand out maps and brochures, and may be able to answer basic questions (locations include the train station's main hall and Gamla Stan). They sell the pricey **City Pass** that covers transportation and a limited number of museums (www.stockholminfo.com).

Stockholm Pass: This pass covers entry to 60 Stockholm sights (including Skansen and the Royal Palace) as well as unlimited City Sightseeing hop-on, hop-off bus/boat tours. It's available in one-day and multiday versions, with an optional Travelcard transit add-on. Prices range from 600 SEK to 1300 SEK (www.stockholmpass.com).

ARRIVAL IN STOCKHOLM
By Train or Bus

Stockholm's adjacent stations for trains (Centralstation) and buses (Cityterminalen), at the southwestern edge of Norrmalm, are a hive of services (including an unofficial Stockholm Info "TI"), eateries, shops, exchange desks, and people on the move. From the train station, the bus station is up the escalators from the main hall and through a glassy atrium (lined with sales desks for bus companies and cruise lines). Those sailing to Estonia or Finland with Tallink Silja (Värtahamnen port) or Viking (Stadsgården port) can catch a shuttle bus from the bus terminal (www. flygbussarna.se). Underground is the T-Centralen subway (T-bana) station—probably the easiest way to reach your hotel. Taxi stands are outside.

The best way to connect the city and its airport is via the Arlanda Express shuttle train, which leaves from tracks 1 and 2 (follow *Arlanda Express/airport train* signs through the station; see below).

By Plane

Arlanda Airport

Stockholm's Arlanda Airport is 28 miles north of town (airport code: ARN, tel. 08/797-6000, www.arlanda.se).

Getting Between the Airport and Downtown: The Arlanda Express **train** is the fastest way to zip between the airport and the central train station. Traveling most of the way at 125 mph, it gets you downtown in just 20 minutes—but it's not cheap (280 SEK one-way, 540 SEK round-trip, free for kids under 17 with adult, covered by rail pass; generally 4-6/hour; tel. 0771/720-200, www.arlandaexpress.com). Buy your ticket either at the window near the track or from a ticket machine, or pay an extra 100 SEK to buy it on board. It's worth checking the website for advance-purchase discounts and two-for-one weekend specials.

Airport shuttle buses (Flygbussarna) run between the airport and Stockholm's train/bus stations (119 SEK, 6/hour, 45 minutes, may take longer at rush hour; buy tickets online—cheapest, from station kiosks, or from 7-Eleven and Pressbyrån convenience stores at the airport and train/bus station, www.flygbussarna.se).

Taxis between the airport and the city center take 30-40 minutes (about 675 SEK, but look for price posted on side of cab). Establish the price first. Most taxis prefer credit cards.

The **cheapest airport connection** is to take bus #583 from the airport to Märsta, then switch to the *pendeltåg* #36 (suburban train, 4-5/hour), which goes to Stockholm's central train station (86 SEK, 1 hour total journey time).

Skavsta Airport

Some discount airlines use Skavsta Airport, about 60 miles south of Stockholm (code: NYO, www.skavsta.se). Flygbussarna shuttle buses connect to the city (159 SEK, cheaper online, 1-2/hour, 80 minutes—but allow extra time for traffic, www.flygbussarna.se).

By Boat

For details on arriving in Stockholm by cruise ship, see "Stockholm Connections" at the end of this chapter.

By Car

Only a Swedish meatball would drive a car in Stockholm. Park it in one of the park-and-ride lots that ring the city and use public transit instead (see lot map at www.visitstockholm.com). Those sailing to Finland or Estonia should ask about long-term parking at the terminal when reserving tickets; to minimize the risk of theft and vandalism, pay extra for the most secure parking garage.

HELPFUL HINTS

Theft Alert: Even in Stockholm, when there are crowds, there are pickpockets (such as at the Royal Palace during the Changing of the Guard). Too-young-to-arrest teens—many from other countries—are hard for local police to control.

Pharmacy: The **C. W. Scheele** 24-hour pharmacy is near the train station at Klarabergsgatan 64 (tel. 08/454-8130).

English Bookstore: The aptly named **English Bookshop** sells a variety of reading materials (including Swedish-interest books) in English (Mon-Fri 11:00-18:30, Sat until 16:00, Sun 12:00-16:00, in the Södermalm district at Södermannag 22, tel. 08/790-5510).

Laundry: Tvättomaten is a rare find—the only self-service independent launderette in Stockholm (48-hour full-service available; open Mon-Fri 8:30-18:30—until 17:00 in July-mid-Aug, Sat 9:30-13:00, closed Sun; across from Gustav Vasa church, Västmannagatan 61 on Odenplan, T-bana: Odenplan, tel. 08/346-480, www.tvattomaten.se).

Museum Admission: Entry to many of Stockholm's fine state-owned museums swings from free (when left-leaning parties control the reins of government) to fee (when center-right parties are in charge). Ask locally for the latest.

GETTING AROUND STOCKHOLM
By Public Transit

Stockholm's fine but pricey public transport network (Stockholm Transport, officially Storstockholms Lokaltrafik—but signed as *SL*) includes subway (Tunnelbana, called "T-bana") and bus systems, and a single handy tram from the commercial center to the sights at Djurgården. It's a spread-out city, so most visitors will need public transport at some point (transit info tel. 08/600-1000, www.sl.se/english). The subway is easy to figure out, but many sights are better served by bus. The main lines are listed on the back of the official city map. A more detailed system map is available free from subway ticket windows, SL Centers (info desks) in main stations, and TIs.

Tickets: A single ride for sub-way, tram, or bus costs 43 SEK (up to 1.25 hours, including transfers); a 24-hour pass is 120 SEK, while a 72-hour pass is 240 SEK. Tickets are sold on the tram (with an extra surcharge), but not on buses. All SL ticket-sellers are clearly marked with a blue flag with the *SL* logo.

Locals and savvy tourists carry a blue **SL-Access card,** which you can buy for 20 SEK at ticket agents, subway and commuter rail stations, and SL Centers. To use the card, just touch it against the blue pad to enter the T-bana turnstile or when boarding a bus or tram. You can add value to the card at station machines or with a ticket agent.

It's still possible to buy single-journey **paper tickets** (at Press-byrån convenience stores inside almost every T-bana station, at self-service machines, and at some transit-ticket offices)—but it's not worth the hassle.

Transit App: SL also has an easy-to-use ticketing app (search "SL-Stockholm" in app stores) that you can tie to a bank card (works with US cards). Buy tickets as you need them on your phone, which you'll then hold to a scanner to enter the T-bana turnstile (or show to a bus/tram driver).

By Harbor Shuttle Ferry

In summer, city ferries let you make a fun, practical, and scenic shortcut across the harbor to Djurgården Island. Boat #82 leaves from the southeast end of Gamla Stan, stops near the Museum of Modern Art on Skeppsholmen, then docks near the Gröna Lund amusement park on Djurgården; boat #80 departs from Nybroplan for Djurgården (43 SEK, covered by public-transit passes, 3-4/hour May-late Sept, 10-minute trip, www.sl.se). The private ferry *Emelie* makes the journey from Nybroplan to Djurgården, landing near the ABBA Museum, then goes on to cruise berth 167 (60 SEK, buy ticket onboard—credit cards only and SL app not valid, hourly, April-Sept roughly Mon-Fri 7:50-18:20, Sat-Sun 9:50-17:50, tel. 08/731-0025, www.ressel.se). While buses and trams run between the same points more frequently, the ferry option gets you out onto the water and can be faster—and certainly more scenic—than overland connections. The hop-on, hop-off boat tour (see "Tours in Stockholm," next) also connects many of these stops.

By Taxi

Stockholm is a good taxi town—provided you find a reputable cab that charges fair rates. Taxis are unregulated, so companies can charge whatever they like. Before hopping in a taxi, look carefully at the big yellow label that should be displayed prominently on the outside of the car (usually in the rear door window). The big number, on the right, shows the "highest unit price" *(högsta järn-förpriset)* for a 10-kilometer ride that lasts 15 minutes; this number should be between 290 and 390 SEK—if it's higher, move on. (You're not obligated to take the first cab in line.) Most cabs charge a drop fee of about 45 SEK. Taxis with inflated rates tend to congregate at touristy places like the Vasa Museum or in Gamla Stan. I've been ripped off enough by cabs here to know: Take only "Taxi Stockholm" cabs with the phone number (08/150-000) printed on the door. (Other reportedly honest companies include Taxi Kurir, tel. 08/300-000, and Taxi 020, tel. 08/850-400 or 020-20-20-20.) Your hotel, restaurant, or museum can call a cab, which will generally arrive within minutes (no extra charge—the meter starts when you hop in).

Tours in Stockholm

The sightseeing company **Strömma** has a lock on most city tours, whether by bus, by boat, or on foot. Their website (www.stromma. se) details the entire program, or you can call for more information (08/1200-4000). Tours can be paid for online, or simply as you board.

BY BUS

Hop-On, Hop-Off Bus Tour

Three hop-on, hop-off buses make a 1.5-hour circuit of the city, orienting riders with a recorded commentary and linking all the essential places from Skansen to City Hall; when cruises are in town, they also stop at both cruise ports (Stadsgården and Frihamnen). **Hop-On Hop-Off**'s green buses and **City Sightseeing**'s red buses both cooperate with Strömma (300 SEK/24 hours, ticket covers both buses; May-Sept 2-3/hour daily 10:00-16:00, fewer off-season, none mid-Jan-mid-Feb, www.stromma.se). **Red Buses** offers a similar hop-on, hop-off itinerary in open-top buses for the same price (3/hour, www.redbuses.se). All offer free Wi-Fi.

Quickie Orientation Bus Tour

Several different city bus tours leave from the Royal Opera House on Gustav Adolfs Torg. Strömma's Stockholm Panorama tour provides a good overview—but, as it's the same price as the 24-hour hop-on, hop-off ticket, I'd take this tour only if you want a quick

STOCKHOLM

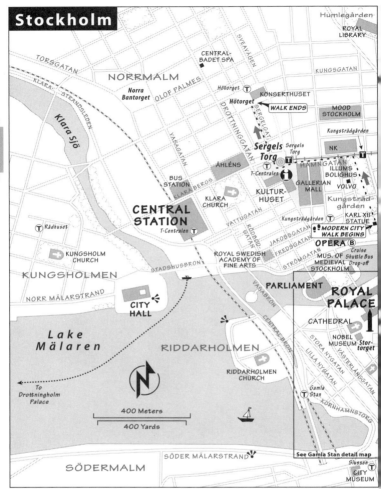

and efficient loop with no unnecessary stops (300 SEK, 4-6/day, fewer Oct-May, 1.25 hours).

BY BOAT
▲City Boat Tours

For a good floating look at Stockholm and a pleasant break, consider a sightseeing cruise. These boat tours are pleasant at the end of the day, when the light is warm and the sights and museums are closed. The handiest are the Strömma/Stockholm Sightseeing boats, which leave from Strömkajen, in front of the Grand Hotel, and stop at Nybroplan five minutes later. The **Royal Canal Tour** is short and informative (200 SEK, 50 minutes, departs at :30 past

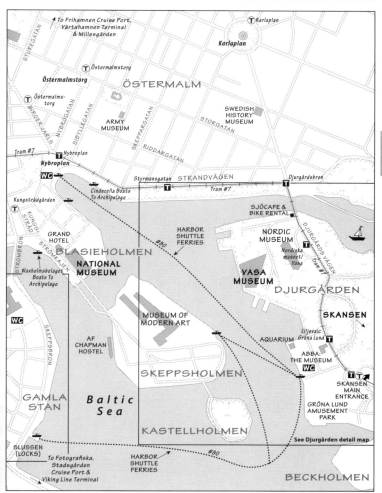

each hour May-Aug 10:30-18:30, less frequent off-season, none Jan-March). The nearly two-hour **Under the Bridges Tour** goes through two locks and under 15 bridges (260 SEK, departures on the hour May-mid-Sept). The **Historic Canal Tour** leaves from the Stadshusbron dock at City Hall (200 SEK, 50 minutes, departs at :30 past the hour June-Aug). You'll circle Kungsholmen island while learning about Stockholm's history from the early Industrial Age to modern times.

Hop-On, Hop-Off Boat Tour

Stockholm is a city surrounded by water, making this boat option enjoyable and practical. Strömma and Red Buses offer the same small loop, stopping at key spots such as Djurgården (Skansen and Vasa Museum), Gamla Stan (near Slussen and again near Royal Palace), the Viking Line dock next to the cruise terminal at Stadsgården, cruise berth 167, and Nybroplan. Use the boat strictly as transport from Point A to Point B, or make the whole one-hour loop and enjoy the recorded commentary (180 SEK/24 hours, 2-3/hour May-mid-Sept, pick up map for schedule and locations of boat stops, www.stromma.se or www.redbuses.se).

ON FOOT

Old Town Walk

Strömma offers a 1.25-hour Old Town walk (180 SEK, July-Aug only at 13:30, departs from ticket booth at north end of Gustav Adolfs Torg, www.stromma.se).

Local Guides

Håkan Fränden is an excellent guide who brings Stockholm to life (mobile 070-531-3379, hakan.franden@hotmail.com). **Marita Bergman** is a teacher and a licensed guide who enjoys showing visitors around during her school breaks (1,650 SEK/half-day tour, mobile 073-511-9154, bergman57.mb@gmail.com). You can also hire a private guide through the Association of Qualified Tourist Guides of Stockholm (www.guidestockholm.com). The standard rate is about 1,650 SEK for up to three hours.

BY BIKE

To tour Stockholm on two wheels, you can either use one of the city's shared bikes or rent your own.

Using City Bikes: Stockholm's City Bikes program is a good option for seeing this bike-friendly town. While you'll find similar bike-sharing programs all over Europe, Stockholm's is the most usable and helpful for travelers. It's easy, the bikes are great, and the city lends itself to joyriding.

Purchase a 165-SEK, three-day City Bike card at the TI, at the SL Center (transit info office) at Sergels Torg, or at many hotels and hostels. The card allows you to grab a bike from one of more than 140 City Bike racks around town. You must return it within three hours (to any rack), but if you want to keep riding, just check out another bike. You can do this over and over for three days (available April-Oct only, www.citybikes.se).

The downside: Unless you have a lock, you can't park your bike as you sightsee. You'll need to return it to a station and get another when you're ready to go—which sounds easy enough, but in practice stations can be full (without an empty port in which to leave a bike) or have no bikes available. To overcome this problem, download City Bike's fun, easy, and free app (search "City Bikes by Clear Channel"), which identifies the nearest racks and bikes.

Renting a Bike: You can also rent bikes (and boats) at the **Sjö-caféet** café, next to Djurgårdsbron bridge near the Vasa Museum. It's ideally situated as a springboard for a pleasant bike ride around the parklike Djurgården island—use their free and excellent bike map/guide. For details, see the Djurgården section under "Sights in Stockholm," later.

Walks in Stockholm

This section includes two different self-guided walks to introduce you to Stockholm, both old (Gamla Stan) and new (the modern city).

▲▲GAMLA STAN WALK

Gamla Stan, Stockholm's historic island old town, is charming, photogenic, and full of antique shops, street lanterns, painted ceilings, and surprises. Until the 1600s, all of Stockholm fit in Gamla Stan. Stockholm traded with other northern ports such as Amsterdam, Lübeck, and Tallinn. German culture influenced art, building styles, and even the language, turning Old Norse into modern Swedish. With its narrow alleys and stairways, Gamla Stan mixes poorly with cars and modern economies. Today, it's been given over to the Royal Palace and to the tourists, who throng Gamla Stan's main drag, Västerlånggatan, seemingly unaware that most of Stockholm's best attractions are elsewhere. While you could just happily wander, this quick walk gives meaning to Stockholm's Old Town.

• *Our walk begins along the harborfront. Start at the base of Slotts-backen (the Palace Hill esplanade) leading up to the...*

Royal Palace: Along the water, check out the ❶ **statue of King Gustav III** gazing at the palace, which was built in the 1700s on the site of Stockholm's first castle (for more about the palace, see the description later in this chapter, under "Sights in Stockholm"). Gustav turned Stockholm from a dowdy Scandinavian port into a sophisticated European capital, modeled on French culture. Gustav loved the arts, and he founded the Royal Dramatic Theater and the Royal Opera in Stockholm. Ironically, he was assassinated by a

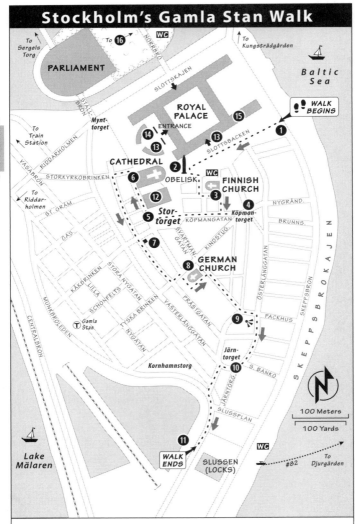

STOCKHOLM

Stockholm's Gamla Stan Walk

To Sergels Torg
To ⑯
NORRBRO
WC
To Kungsträdgården

PARLIAMENT

SLOTTSKAJEN

ROYAL PALACE

B a l t i c
S e a

WALK BEGINS

Mynt-torget

STALLBRON

⑭ ENTRANCE
⑮
⑬

To Train Station

RIDDARHOLMEN

⑬
SLOTTSBACKEN
①

VASABRON

CATHEDRAL

STORKYRKOBRINKEN

② OBELISK

WC
FINNISH CHURCH

③

④
Köpman-torget

NYGRÄND

To Riddar-holmen

ST. GRÄM

⑥

⑫

Stor-torget
⑤

KÖPMANGATAN

BRUNNS.

GAS.

SVARTMAN-GATAN

KINDSTU.

ÖSTERLÅNGGATAN

SKEPPSBROKAJEN

⑦

GERMAN CHURCH
⑧

KÅKBRINKEN

STORA NYGATAN

SCHÖNFELTS

LILLA

PRÄSTGATAN

VÄSTERLÅNGGATAN

⑨

PACKHUS

CENTRALBRON

MUNKBROLEDEN

Ⓣ Gamla Stan

TYSKA BRINKEN

NYGATAN

Kornhamnstorg

Järn-torget
⑩

S. BANKO

JÄRNTORG.

N

Lake Mälaren

⑪
WALK ENDS

SLUSSPLAN

100 Meters
100 Yards

WC

#82
To Djurgården

SLUSSEN (LOCKS)

Walk

① King Gustav III Statue
② Obelisk
③ Iron Boy Statue
④ St. George Statue
⑤ Stortorget
⑥ Cathedral
⑦ Rune Stone
⑧ German Church
⑨ Viewpoint
⑩ Järntorget
⑪ Bridge & Lock

Additional Sights

⑫ Nobel Museum
⑬ Palace Tickets (2)
⑭ Changing of the Guard
⑮ Royal Armory
⑯ To Museum of Medieval Stockholm

discontented nobleman, who shot Gustav in the back at a masquerade ball at the Royal Opera House in 1792 (inspiring Verdi's opera *Un Ballo in Maschera*).

Walk up the broad, cobbled boulevard alongside the palace to the crest of the hill. Stop, look back, and scan the harbor. The grand building across the water is the National Museum, which is often mistaken for the palace. Beyond that, in the distance, is the fine row of buildings on Strandvägen street. Until the 1850s, this area was home to peasant shacks, but as Stockholm entered its grand stage, it

was cleaned up and replaced by fine apartments, including some of the city's smartest addresses. A blocky gray TV tower stands tall in the distance. Turn to the palace facade on your left (finished in 1754, replacing one that burned in 1697). The niches are filled with Swedish bigwigs (literally) from the mid-18th century.

As you crest the hill, you're facing the ❷ **obelisk** that honors Stockholm's merchant class for its support in a 1788 war against

Russia. In front of the obelisk are tour buses (their drivers worried about parking cops) and a pit used for *boules*. The royal family took a liking to the French game during a Mediterranean vacation, and it's quite popular around town today.

Behind the obelisk stands Storkyrkan, Stockholm's cathedral (which we'll visit later on this walk). From this angle you can see its Baroque facade, which was added to better match the newer palace. Opposite the boules court and palace is the Finnish church (Finska Kyrkan, the deep orange building), which originated as the royal tennis hall. When the Protestant Reformation hit in 1527, church services could at last be said in the peoples' languages rather than Latin. Suddenly, each merchant community needed its own church. Finns worshipped here, the Germans built their own church (coming up on this walk), and the Swedes got the cathedral.

Stroll up the lane to the right of the Finnish church into the shady churchyard, where you'll find the fist-sized ❸ *Iron Boy,* the tiniest public statue (out of about 600 statues) in Stockholm. Swedish grannies knit caps for him in the winter. Local legend says the statue honors the orphans who had to transfer cargo from sea ships to lake ships before Stockholm's locks were built. Some people rub

STOCKHOLM

his head for good luck (which the orphans didn't have). Others, perhaps needy when it comes to this gift, rub his head for wisdom. The artist says it's simply a self-portrait of himself as a child, sitting on his bed and gazing at the moon.

• *Exit through either of the churchyard gates, turn left onto Trädgårdsgatan, then bear right with the lane until you pop out at...*

Köpmangatan: Take a moment to explore this street from one end to the other. With its cobbles and traditional pastel facades, this is a quintessential Gamla Stan lane—and one of the oldest in town. The mellow yellow houses are predominantly from the 18th century; the reddish facades are mostly 17th century. Once merchants' homes, today these are popular with antique dealers and refined specialty shops. Back when there was comfort living within a city's walls, Gamla Stan streets like this were densely populated.

If you head left, you'll emerge on Köpmantorget square, with the breathtaking ❹ **statue of St. George** slaying the dragon, with a maiden representing Stockholm (about 10 steps to the right) looking on with thanks and admiration. If you go right, you'll reach old Stockholm's main square, our next stop.

❺ **Stortorget:** Colorful old buildings topped with gables line this square—Stockholm's oldest. In 1400, this was the heart

of medieval Stockholm (pop. 6,000). Here at the town well, many tangled lanes intersected, making it the natural center for trading. Today Stortorget is home to lots of tourists—including a steady storm of cruise groups following the numbered Ping-Pong paddle of their guides on four-hour blitz tours of the city (300 ships call here between June and September). The square also hosts concerts, occasional demonstrators, and—in winter—Christmas shoppers at an outdoor market.

The grand building on the right is the old stock exchange, now home to the noble **Nobel Museum** (described under "Sights in Stockholm"), although it may move by the time you visit. On the immediate left is the social-services agency **Stockholms Stadsmission** (offering the cheapest and best lunch around at the recommended Grillska Huset). If you peek into the adjacent bakery, you'll get a fine look at the richly decorated ceilings characteristic of Gamla Stan in the 17th century—the exotic flowers and animals implied that the people who lived or worked here were worldly. You'll also spy some tempting marzipan cakes (a local favorite) and *kanelbullar* (cinnamon buns). There's a cheap sandwich counter in the back and lots of picnic benches in the square.

The town well is still a popular meeting point. This square long held the town's pillory. Scan the fine old facades. The site of the **Stockholm Bloodbath** of 1520, this square has a notorious history. During a Danish power grab, many of Stockholm's movers and shakers who had challenged Danish rule—Swedish aristocracy, leading merchants, and priests—were rounded up, brought here, and beheaded. Rivers of blood were said to have flowed through the streets. Legend holds that the 80 or so white stones in the fine red facade across the square symbolize the victims. (One victim's son escaped, went into hiding, and resurfaced to lead a Swedish revolt against the Danish rulers. Three years later, the Swedes elected that rebel, Gustav Vasa, as their first king. He went on to usher in a great period in the country's history—the Swedish Renaissance.)
• *At the far end of the square (under the finest gables), turn right and follow Trångsund toward the cathedral.*

❻ Cathedral (Storkyrkan): Just before the yellow-brick church, you'll see my personal phone booth (Rikstelefon) and the gate to

the churchyard—guarded by statues of Caution and Hope. Enter the church—Stockholm's oldest, from the 13th century (60 SEK, daily 9:00-16:00). Signs explain special events, as this church is busy with tours and services in summer.

When buying your ticket, pick up the free, worthwhile English-language flier. Exploring the cathedral's interior, you'll find many styles, ranging from medieval to modern. The front of the nave is paved with centuries-old **tombstones.** The tombstone of the Swedish reformer Olaus Petri is appropriately simple and appropriately located—under the finely carved and gilded pulpit on the left side of the nave. A witness to the Stockholm Bloodbath, Petri was nearly executed himself. He went on to befriend Gustav Vasa and guide him in Lutheranizing Sweden (and turning this cathedral from Catholic to Protestant).

Opposite the pulpit, find the **bronze plaque** in the pillar. It recalls the 1925 Swedish-led ecumenical meeting of Christian leaders that encouraged all churches to renew their efforts on behalf of peace and justice, especially given the horrific toll of World War I.

Next, the best seats in the house: the carved wood **royal boxes,** dating from 1684. This has been a royal wedding church throughout the ages. It was here, in June 2010, that Crown Princess Victoria, heir to the throne, married Daniel Westling (her personal trainer) with much pomp and ceremony.

The fine 17th-century **altar** is made of silver and ebony. Above it, the silver Christ stands like a conquering general evoking the 1650s, an era of Swedish military might.

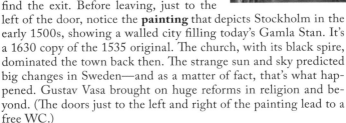

Next to the altar is a wondrous 1489 statue, carved from oak and elk horn, of **St. George** slaying the dragon (we saw a copy of it outside a few minutes ago). To some, this symbolizes the Swedes overcoming the evil Danes (commemorating a military victory in 1471). In a broader sense, it's an inspiration to take up the struggle against even non-Danish evil. Regardless, it must be the gnarliest dragon's head in all of Europe.

Return to the back of the church to find the exit. Before leaving, just to the left of the door, notice the **painting** that depicts Stockholm in the early 1500s, showing a walled city filling today's Gamla Stan. It's a 1630 copy of the 1535 original. The church, with its black spire, dominated the town back then. The strange sun and sky predicted big changes in Sweden—and as a matter of fact, that's what happened. Gustav Vasa brought on huge reforms in religion and beyond. (The doors just to the left and right of the painting lead to a free WC.)

Heading outside, you'll emerge into the kid-friendly churchyard, which was once the cemetery.

• *With your back to the church's front door, go right. At the next corner, turn left (on Storkyrkobrinken), then left again on...*

Prästgatan: Enjoy a quiet wander down this peaceful 15th-century "Priests' Lane." Västerlånggatan, the touristy drag, parallels this lane one block over. (While we'll skip it now, you can walk back up it from the end point of this walk.) As you stroll Prästgatan, look for bits of its past: hoists poking out horizontally from gables (merchants used these to lift goods into their attics), tie bolts (iron bars necessary to bind the timber beams of tall buildings together), small coal or wood hatches (for fuel delivery back in the good old days), and flaming gold phoenixes under red-crown medallions (telling firefighters which houses paid insurance and could be saved in case of fire—for example, #46). Like other Scandinavian cities, Stockholm was plagued by fire until it was finally decreed that only stone, stucco, and brick construction (like you see here) would be allowed in the town center.

After a few blocks (at Kåkbrinken), a cannon barrel on the corner (look down) guards a Viking-age ❼ **rune stone.** In case you can't read the old Nordic script, it says: "Torsten and Frogun erected this stone in memory of their son."

• *Continue one block farther down Prästgatan to Tyska Brinken and turn left. Look up to see the powerful brick steeple of the...*

❽ **German Church** (Tyska Kyrkan): The church's carillon has played four times a day since 1666. Think of the days when German merchants worked here. Today, Germans come to Sweden not to run the economy, but to enjoy its pristine nature (which is progressively harder to find in their own crowded homeland). Sweden formally became a Lutheran country even before the northern part of Germany—making this the very first German Lutheran church (free to enter).

• *Wander through the churchyard (past a cute church café) and out the back. Exit right onto Svartmangatan and follow it to the right, ending at an iron railing overlooking Österlånggatan.*

❾ **Viewpoint:** From this perch, survey the street below to the left and right. Notice how it curves. This marks the old shoreline. In medieval times, piers stretched out like fingers into the harbor. Gradually, as land was reclaimed and developed, these piers were extended, becoming lanes leading to piers farther away. Behind you is a cute shop where elves can actually be seen making elves.

• *Walk right to Österlånggatan, and continue on to...*

❿ **Järntorget:** A customs square in medieval times, this was the home of Sweden's first bank back in 1680 (the yellow building with the bars on the windows). The Co-op Nära supermarket on this square offers picnic fixings. From here, Västerlånggatan—the eating, shopping, and commercial pedestrian mall of Gamla Stan—leads back across the island. You'll be there in a minute, but first finish this walk.

• *Continue from the square (opposite where you entered) down Järntorgsgatan until you emerge (suddenly) into traffic hell. For now, things are a bit of a mess because of an enormous redevelopment project that will eventually turn this area into a green people-zone. Let's continue ahead, crossing over the busy street to reach a viewpoint window (cut into the construction wall that lines the bridge).*

⓫ **Bridge Overlooking Slussen:** This area is called Slussen, named for the locks between the salt water of the Baltic Sea (to your left) and the fresh water of the huge **Lake Mälaren** (to your right). In fact, Stockholm exists because this is where Lake Mälaren meets the sea. Traders would sail their goods from far inland to this point, where they'd meet merchants who would ship the goods south to Europe. In the 13th century, the new kingdom of Sweden needed revenue, and began levying duty taxes on all the iron, copper, and furs shipped through here.

From the bridge, you may notice a current in the water, indicating that the weir has been lowered and water is spilling from Lake Mälaren (about two feet above sea level) into the sea. Today, the locks are nicknamed "the divorce lock" because this is where captains and first mates learn to communicate under pressure and in the public eye.

Opposite Gamla Stan is the island of **Södermalm**—bohemian, youthful, artsy, and casual—with its popular Katarina viewing platform (see "Stockholm's Best Views" sidebar, later). Moored on the saltwater side are cruise ships, which bring thousands of visitors into town each day during the season. Many of these boats are bound for Finland. The towering white syringe is the Gröna Lund amusement park's free-fall ride. The revolving *Djurgården Färjan* sign, along the embankment to your left, marks the ferry that zips from here directly to Gröna Lund and Djurgården.

• *Our walk is finished, but feel free to linger longer in Gamla Stan—day or night, it's a lively place to enjoy.* **Västerlånggatan,** *Gamla Stan's main commercial drag, is a touristy festival of distractions that keeps most visitors from seeing the historic charms of the Old Town—which you just did. Now you're free to window-shop and eat (see "Shopping in Stockholm" and "Eating in Stockholm," later). Or, if it's late, find some live music (see "Nightlife and Entertainment in Stockholm").*

For more sightseeing, consider the other sights in **Gamla Stan** *or at the* **Royal Palace** *(all described under "Sights in Stockholm"). Or backtrack to Västerlånggatan (always going straight), to reach the parliament building and cross the water back over onto Norrmalm (where the street becomes Drottninggatan). This pedestrian street leads back into Stockholm's modern town.*

Yet another option is to walk 15 minutes to **Kungsträdgården,** *the starting point of my "Stockholm's Modern City" self-guided walk. Either walk along the embankment and take the diagonal bridge directly across to the square, or walk back through the middle of Gamla Stan, take the stately walkway past the Swedish Parliament building, then turn right when you cross the bridge.*

STOCKHOLM'S MODERN CITY WALK

On this walk, we'll use the park called Kungsträdgården as a springboard to explore the modern center of Stockholm—a commercial zone that puts the focus not on old kings and mementos of

Fika: **Sweden's Coffee Break**

Swedes drink more coffee per capita than just about any other country in the world. The Swedish coffee break—or *fika*—is a ritual. *Fika* is to Sweden what teatime is to Britain. The typical *fika* is a morning or afternoon break in the workday, but can happen any time, any day. It's the perfect opportunity (and excuse) for tourists to take a break as well.

Fika fare is coffee with a snack—something sweet or savory. Your best bet is a *kanelbulle*, a Swedish cinnamon bun, although some prefer *pariserbulle*, a bun filled with vanilla cream. These can be found nearly everywhere coffee is sold, including just about any café or *konditori* (bakery) in Stockholm. A coffee and a cinnamon bun in a café will cost you about 40 SEK. (Most cafés will give you a coffee refill for free.) But at Pressbyrån, the Swedish convenience stores found all over town, you can satisfy your *fika* fix for 25 SEK by getting a coffee and bun to go. Grab a park bench or waterside perch, relax, and enjoy.

superpower days, but on shopping. For the route, see the "Stockholm" map.

• *Find the statue of King Karl XII, facing the waterfront at the harbor end of the park.*

Kungsträdgården: Centuries ago, this "King's Garden" was the private kitchen garden of the king, where he grew his cabbage

salad. Today, this downtown people-watching center, worth ▲, is considered Stockholm's living room, symbolizing the Swedes' freedom-loving spirit. While the name implies that the garden is a private royal domain, the giant clump of elm trees just behind the statue reminds locals that it's the people who rule now. In the 1970s, demonstrators chained themselves to these trees to stop the building of an underground train station here. They prevailed, and today, locals enjoy the peaceful, breezy ambience of a teahouse instead.

Farther on, watch for the AstroTurf zone with "latte dads" and their kids, and enjoy a summer concert at the bandstand. There's always something going on. High above is a handy reference point—the revolving NK clock.

Kungsträdgården—surrounded by the harborfront and tour boats, the Royal Opera House, and shopping opportunities (including a welcoming Volvo showroom near the top-left side of the square, showing off the latest in Swedish car design)—is *the* place to feel Stockholm's pulse (but always ask first: *"Kan jag kanna på din puls?"*).

The garden also plays host to huge parties. The Taste of Stockholm festival runs for a week in early June, when restaurateurs show off and bands entertain all day. Beer flows liberally—a rare public spectacle in Sweden.

• *Stroll through Kungsträdgården, past the fountain and the Volvo store, and up to Hamngatan street. From here, we'll turn left and walk the length of the NK department store (across the street) as we wade through...*

Stockholm's Urban Shopping Zone (Hamngatan): In just a couple of blocks, we'll pass some major landmarks of Swedish consumerism. First, anchoring the corner at the top of Kungsträdgården, is the gigantic **Illums Bolighus** design shop. (You can enter from the square and stroll all the way through it, popping out at Hamngatan on the far end.) This is a Danish institution, making its play for Swedish customers with this prime location. Across the street, notice the giant gold *NK* marking the **Nordiska Kompaniet** department store (locals joke that the NK stands for "no kronor left"). It's located in an elegant early-20th-century building that dominates the top end of Kungsträdgården. If it feels like an old-time American department store, that's because its architect was inspired by grand stores he'd seen in the US (circa 1910).

Another block down, on the left, is the sleeker, more modern **Gallerian mall.** Among this two-story world of shops, upstairs you'll find a Clas Ohlson hardware and electronics shop (most Stockholmers have a cabin that's always in need of a little DIY repair). And there are plenty of affordable little lunch bars and classy cafés for your *fika* (Swedish coffee-and-bun break). You may notice that American influence (frozen yogurt and other trendy food chains) is challenging the notion of the traditional *fika.*

• *High-end shoppers should consider heading into the streets behind NK, with exclusive designer boutiques and the chichi Mood Stockholm mall (see "Shopping in Stockholm," later). Otherwise, just beyond the huge Gallerian mall, you'll emerge into Sergels Torg. (Note that the handy tram #7 goes from here directly to Skansen and the other important sights on Djurgården; departures every few minutes.)*

Sergels Torg and Kulturhuset: Sergels Torg square, worth ▲, dominates the heart of modern Stockholm with its stark 1960s-era functionalist architecture. The glassy tower in the middle of the fountain plaza is ugly in daylight but glows at night, symbolic of Sweden's haunting northern lights.

Kulturhuset, the hulking, low-slung, glassy building overlooking the square, is Stockholm's "culture center"—a public space for everyone in Stockholm. In this lively cultural zone, there are libraries, theater, a space for kids, chessboards, fun shops, fine art cinema, art exhibits, and a music venue (tel. 08/5062-0200, http://kulturhusetstadsteatern.se).

I like to take the elevator to the top of the Kulturhuset and explore each level by riding the escalator back down to the ground floor. On the rooftop, the recommended Cafeteria Panorama has cheap meals and a salad bar with terrific city views.

Back at ground level outside, stand in front of the Kulturhuset (across from the fountain) and survey the expansive square nicknamed "Plattan" (the platter). Everything around you dates from the 1960s and 1970s, when this formerly run-down area was reinvented as an urban "space of the future." In the 1970s, with no nearby residences, the desolate Plattan became the domain of junkies. Now the city is actively revitalizing it, and the Plattan is becoming a people-friendly heart of the commercial town.

DesignTorget (enter from the lower level of Kulturhuset) showcases practical items for everyday use from established and emerging designers. Nearby are the major boutiques and department stores, including, across the way, H&M and Åhléns.

Sergelgatan, a thriving pedestrian and commercial street, leads past the five uniform white towers you see beyond the fountain. These office towers, so modern in the 1960s, have gone from seeming hopelessly out-of-date to being considered "retro," and are now quite popular with young professionals.

• *Walk up Sergelgatan past the towers, enjoying the public art and people-watching, to the market at Hötorget.*

Hötorget: "Hötorget" means "Hay Market," but today its stalls feed people rather than horses. The adjacent indoor market,

Hötorgshallen, is fun and fragrant. It dates from 1914 when, for hygienic reasons, the city forbade selling fish and meat outdoors. Carl Milles' statue of *Orpheus Emerging from the Underworld* (with seven sad Muses) stands in front of the city concert hall (which hosts the annual Nobel Prize award ceremony). The concert house, from 1926, is Swedish Art Deco (a.k.a. "Swedish Grace"). The lobby (open through much of the summer) still evokes Stockholm's

Roaring Twenties. If the door's open, you're welcome to look in for free.

Popping into the Hötorget T-bana station provides a fun glimpse at local urban design. Stockholm's subway system was inaugurated in the 1950s, and many stations are modern art installations in themselves.

• *Our walk ends here. For more shopping and an enjoyable pedestrian boulevard leading back into the Old Town, cut down a block to Drottninggatan and turn left. This busy drag leads straight out of the commercial district, passes the parliament, then becomes the main street of Gamla Stan.*

Sights in Stockholm

GAMLA STAN (OLD TOWN)
The best of this island is covered in my "Gamla Stan" self-guided walk, earlier. But here are a few ways to extend your time in the Old Town.

On Stortorget
▲Nobel Museum (Nobelmuseet)
Opened in 2001 for the 100-year anniversary of the Nobel Prize, this wonderful little museum tells the story of the world's most

prestigious prize. Pricey but high-tech and eloquent, it fills the grand old stock exchange building that dominates Gamla Stan's main square, Stortorget. By the time you visit, the museum may have relocated to a new building on Blasieholmen—inquire locally.

Cost and Hours: 120 SEK, free Tue after 17:00; daily 9:00-20:00; Sept-May Tue-Fri 11:00-17:00, Tue until 20:00, Sat-Sun 10:00-18:00, closed Mon; audioguide-20 SEK, free 40-minute orientation tours in English—check website for times, tel. 08/5348-1800, www.nobelmuseum.se.

Background: Stockholm-born Alfred Nobel was a great inventor, with more than 300 patents. His most famous invention: dynamite. Living in the late 1800s, Nobel was a man of his age. It was a time of great optimism, wild ideas, and grand projects. His dynamite enabled entire nations to blast their way into the modern age with canals, railroads, and tunnels. It made warfare much more destructive. And it also made Alfred Nobel a very wealthy man. Wanting to leave a legacy that celebrated and supported people with great ideas, Alfred used his fortune to fund the Nobel Prize. Every year since 1901, laureates have been honored in the fields of physics, chemistry, medicine, literature, economic sciences, and peacemaking.

Visiting the Museum: Inside, portraits of all 700-plus prize-winners hang from the ceiling—shuffling around the room like shirts at the dry cleaner's (miss your favorite, and he or she will come around again in six hours). Behind the ticket desk are monitors that represent the six Nobel Prize categories, each honoring the most recent laureate in that category.

Flanking the main hall beyond that—where touchscreens organized by decade invite you to learn more about the laureates of your choice—two rooms run a continuous video montage of quick programs (on one side, films celebrating the creative milieus that encouraged Nobel laureates past and present; on the other side, short films about their various paths to success).

To the right of the ticket desk, find "The Gallery," with a surprisingly captivating collection of items that various laureates have cited as important to their creative process, from scientific equipment to inspirational knickknacks. The randomness of the items offers a fascinating and humanizing insight into the great minds of our time.

The Viennese-style Bistro Nobel is the place to get creative with your coffee...and sample the famous Nobel ice cream. All Nobel laureates who visit the museum are asked to sign the bottom of a chair in the café. Turn yours over and see who warmed your chair. And don't miss the lockable hangers, to protect your fancy, furry winter coat. The Swedish Academy, which awards the Nobel Prize for literature each year, is upstairs.

Royal Palace Complex (Kungliga Slottet)

Although the royal family beds down at Drottningholm (see next chapter), this complex in Gamla Stan is still the official royal residence. The palace, designed in Italian Baroque style, was completed in 1754 after a fire wiped out the previous palace—a much more characteristic medieval/Renaissance complex. This blocky Baroque replacement, which houses various museums, is big and (frankly) pretty dull. See the "Gamla Stan Walk" map to sort out the various entrances.

Planning Your Time: Visiting the several sights in and near the palace could fill a day, but Stockholm has far better attractions elsewhere. Prioritize.

Visitors in a rush should see the Changing of the Guard, enter the (free) Royal Armory—if it's open when you visit, and skip the rest. Information booths in the semicircular courtyard (at the top, where the guard changes) and just inside the east entry give out a

Stockholm at a Glance

▲▲▲**Skansen** Europe's first and best open-air folk museum, with more than 150 old homes, churches, shops, and schools. **Hours:** Park-opens daily at 10:00, closes at 22:00 late June-Aug and progressively earlier the rest of the year; historical buildings-generally 11:00-17:00, late June-Aug some until 19:00, most closed in winter. See page 48.

▲▲▲**Vasa Museum** Ill-fated 17th-century warship dredged from the sea floor, now the showpiece of an interesting museum. **Hours:** Daily 8:30-18:00; Sept-May 10:00-17:00 except Wed until 20:00. See page 50.

▲▲**Military Parade and Changing of the Guard** Punchy pomp starting near Nybroplan and finishing at Royal Palace outer courtyard. **Hours:** Late April-Aug daily, Sept-late April Wed and Sat-Sun only, start time varies with season but always at midday. See page 36.

▲▲**Royal Armory** A fine collection of ceremonial medieval royal armor, historic and modern royal garments, and carriages, in the Royal Palace (most of museum may be closed for renovation when you visit). **Hours:** Daily May-June 11:00-17:00, July-Aug 10:00-18:00; Sept-April Tue-Sun 11:00-17:00, Thu until 20:00, closed Mon. See page 37.

▲▲**City Hall** Gilt mosaic architectural jewel of Stockholm and site of Nobel Prize banquet, with tower offering the city's best views. **Hours:** Required tours daily generally June-Aug every 30 minutes 9:30-15:30, fewer off-season. See page 40.

▲▲**Swedish History Museum** Collection of artifacts spanning Sweden's entire history, highlighted by fascinating Viking exhibit and Gold Room. **Hours:** Daily 10:00-17:00; Sept-May closed Mon and open Wed until 20:00. See page 44.

▲**Nordic Museum** Danish Renaissance palace design and five fascinating centuries of traditional Swedish lifestyles. **Hours:** Daily 9:00-18:00; Sept-May 10:00-17:00 except Wed until 20:00. See page 52.

list of the day's guided tours and an explanatory brochure/map that marks the entrances to the different sights. The main entrance to the Royal Palace (including the apartments, chapel, and treasury) faces the long, angled square and obelisk (but you can cut through the palace's interior courtyard to get there).

The Royal Palace ticket includes four museums. Of these, the

▲**Nobel Museum** Star-studded tribute to some of the world's most accomplished scientists, artists, economists, and politicians. **Hours:** Daily 9:00-20:00; Sept-May Tue-Fri 11:00-17:00, Tue until 20:00, Sat-Sun 10:00-18:00, closed Mon. See page 32.

▲**Royal Palace Museums** Complex of Swedish royal museums, the two best of which are the Royal Apartments and Royal Treasury. **Hours:** Daily 10:00-17:00, July-Aug from 9:00; Oct-April until 16:00 and closed Mon. See page 37.

▲**Kungsträdgården** Stockholm's lively central square, with life-size chess games, concerts, and perpetual action. See page 29.

▲**Sergels Torg** Modern square with underground mall. See page 30.

▲**ABBA: The Museum** A super-commercial and wildly-popular-with-ABBA-fans experience. **Hours:** Daily 9:00-19:00; Sept-May daily 10:00-18:00 except Wed until 19:00. See page 54.

▲**Thielska Galleriet** Enchanting waterside mansion with works of Scandinavian artists Larsson, Zorn, and Munch. **Hours:** Tue-Sun 12:00-17:00, closed Mon. See page 56.

▲**Fotografiska** Fun photography museum focusing on contemporary and international work, with eye-popping views from its top-floor café. **Hours:** Daily 9:00-23:00, later on weekends. See page 57.

▲**Millesgården** Dramatic cliffside museum and grounds featuring works of Sweden's greatest sculptor, Carl Milles. **Hours:** Daily 11:00-17:00 except closed Mon Oct-April. See page 58.

▲**Museum of Medieval Stockholm** Underground museum shows off parts of town wall King Gustav Vasa built in 1530s. **Hours:** Tue-Sun 12:00-17:00, Wed until 19:00, closed Mon. See page 39.

Royal Apartments are not much as far as palace rooms go but still worthwhile; the Royal Treasury is worth a look; the Museum of Three Crowns gets you down into the medieval cellars to learn about the more interesting earlier castle; and Gustav III's Museum of Antiquities is skippable. The chapel is nice enough (and it's free to enter).

Tours: In peak season, the main Royal Palace offers a full slate of English tours covering the different sights (included in admission)—allowing you to systematically cover nearly the entire complex. If you're paying the hefty price for a ticket, you might as well join at least one of the tours—otherwise, you'll struggle to appreciate the place. Some tours are infrequent, so be sure to confirm times when you purchase your admission (for more on tours, see the individual listings below).

Expect Changes: Since the palace is used for state functions, it's sometimes closed to tourists. And, as the exterior is undergoing a 20-year renovation, don't be surprised if parts are covered in scaffolding. Most of the Royal Armory is closed for renovation, while the Royal Coin Cabinet has closed and will reopen in a new location in Östermalm in a few years.

▲▲Military Parade and Changing of the Guard

Starting from the Army Museum (two blocks from Nybroplan at Riddargatan 13), Stockholm's daily military parade marches

over Norrbro bridge, in front of the parliament building, and up to the Royal Palace's outer courtyard, where the band plays and the guard changes. Smaller contingents of guards spiral in from other parts of the palace complex, eventually convening in the same place.

The performance is fresh and spirited, because the soldiers are visiting Stockholm just like you—and it's a chance for young soldiers from all over Sweden in every branch of the service to show their stuff in the big city. Pick your place at the palace courtyard, where the band arrives at about 12:15 (13:15 on Sun). The best spot to stand is along the wall in the inner courtyard, near the palace information and ticket office. There are columns with wide pedestals for easy perching, as well as benches that people stand on to view the ceremony (arrive early). Generally, after the barking and goose-stepping formalities, the band shows off for an impressive 30-minute marching concert.

Marching Band and Parade: Departs from Army Museum late April-Aug Mon-Sat at 11:45, Sun at 12:45 (11:35 and 12:35, respectively, if departing from Cavalry Barracks); Sept-Oct Wed and Sat at 11:45,

Sun at 12:45; off-season departs from Mynttorget Wed and Sat at 12:09, Sun at 13:09. Royal appointments can disrupt the schedule; confirm times at TI. In summer, you might also catch the mounted guards (they don't appear on a regular schedule).

Royal Guards Ceremony at the Palace: Mon-Sat at 12:15, Sun at 13:15, about 40 minutes, in front of the Royal Palace. You can get details at www.forsvarsmakten.se (click on "Activities").

▲▲Royal Armory (Livrustkammaren)

The oldest museum in Sweden is both more and less than an armory. Rather than dusty piles of swords and muskets, it focuses on royal clothing: impressive ceremonial armor (never used in battle) and other fashion through the ages (including a room of kidswear), plus a fine collection of coaches. It's an engaging slice of royal life. Everything is displayed under sturdy brick vaults, beautifully lit, and well-described in English and by a good audioguide. The museum has undertaken a major renovation that closed the main exhibit halls, but the lower level, with a good display of royal coaches, remains open.

Cost and Hours: Free; daily May-June 11:00-17:00, July-Aug 10:00-18:00; Sept-April Tue-Sun 11:00-17:00, Thu until 20:00, closed Mon; audioguide-40 SEK, information sheets in English available in most rooms; entrance at bottom of Slottsbacken at base of palace, tel. 08/402-3010, www.livrustkammaren.se.

▲Royal Palace

The Royal Palace consists of a chapel (free) and four museums. Compared to many grand European palaces, it's underwhelming and flooded with cruise-excursion groups who don't realize that Stockholm's best sightseeing is elsewhere.

Cost and Hours: 160-SEK combo-ticket covers all four museums, includes guided tours; daily 10:00-17:00, July-Aug from 9:00; Oct-April until 16:00 and closed Mon; tel. 08/402-6130, www.royalcourt.se.

Orientation: I've listed the museums in order of sightseeing worthiness. But if you want to see them all with minimal backtracking, follow this plan: Begin at the entrance on Slottsbacken. Head up to the chapel for a peek, then descend to the treasury. Tour the Royal Apartments, exiting at the far side of the building—where you can head straight into the Museum of Three Crowns. Exiting there, you'll find the final sight (Museum of Antiquities) to your right.

Royal Apartments: The stately palace exterior encloses 608 rooms (one more than Britain's Buckingham Palace) of glittering 18th-century Baroque and Rococo decor. Guided 45-minute tours in English run twice daily (at 10:30 and 13:30).

Clearly the palace of Scandinavia's superpower, it's steeped in royal history. You'll enter the grand main hall (cheapskates can get a free look at this first room before reaching the ticket checkpoint), then walk the long halls through four sections. On the main level are the Hall of State (with an exhibit of fancy state awards) and the lavish Bernadotte Apartments (some fine Rococo interiors and portraits of the Bernadotte dynasty); upstairs you'll find the State Apartments (with rooms dating to the 1690s—darker halls, faded tapestries, and a wannabe hall of mirrors) and the Guest Apartments (with less lavish quarters, where visiting heads of state still crash).

Royal Treasury (Skattkammaren): Refreshingly compact compared to the sprawling apartments, the treasury gives you a good, up-close look at Sweden's crown jewels. It's particularly worthwhile with an English guided tour (daily at 11:30) or the included audioguide (which covers basically the same information).

Climbing down into the super-secure vault, you'll see 12 cases filled with fancy crowns, scepters, jeweled robes, the silver baptismal font of Karl XI, and plenty of glittering gold. The first room holds the crowns of princes and princesses, while the second shows off the more serious regalia of kings and queens. For more than a century, these crowns have gone unworn: The last Swedish coronation was Oskar II's in 1873; in 1907 his son and successor—out of deference for the constitution (and living in a Europe that was deep in the throes of modernism)—declined to wear the crown, so he was "enthroned" rather than "coronated." The crowns still belong to the monarchs and are present in the room on special occasions—but they are symbols rather than accessories.

Museum of Three Crowns (Museum Tre Kronor): This museum shows off bits of the palace from before a devastating 1697 fire (guided tours in English offered at 11:30). The models, illustrations, and artifacts are displayed in vaulted medieval cellars that are far more evocative than the run-of-the-mill interior of today's palace. But while the stroll through the cellars is atmospheric, it's basically just more old stuff, interesting only to real history buffs.

Royal Chapel: If you don't want to spring for a ticket, but would like a little taste of palace opulence, climb the stairs inside the main entrance for a peek into the chapel. It's standard-issue royal Baroque: colorful ceiling painting, bubbly altars, and a giant organ.

Gustav III's Museum of Antiquities (Gustav III's Antikmuseum): In the 1700s, Gustav III traveled through Italy and brought home an impressive gallery of classical Roman statues. These are displayed exactly as they were in the 1790s. This was a huge deal for those who had never been out of Sweden.

▲Royal Coin Cabinet (Kungliga Myntkabinettet)

More than your typical royal coin collection, this is the best money museum I've seen in Europe. But it's being relocated (to a space at the Swedish History Museum), and won't be displaying its coins and banknotes again for a few years. For the latest, consult the museum website (www.myntkabinettet.se).

More Gamla Stan Sights

These first two sights sit on the Gamla Stan islet of Helgeandshol-men (just north of the Royal Palace), which is dominated by the Swedish Parliament building. Also at the edge of Gamla Stan is the stately island of Riddarholmen.

Parliament (Riksdag)

For a firsthand look at Sweden's government, tour the parliament buildings. Guides enjoy a chance to teach a little Swedish poli-sci along the standard tour of the building and its art. It's also possible to watch the parliament in session.

Cost and Hours: Free one-hour tours go in English late June-mid-Aug, usually 4/day Mon-Fri (when parliament is not in session). The rest of the year tours run 1/day Sat-Sun only; you're also welcome to join Swedish citizens in the viewing gallery (free); enter at Riksgatan 3a, call 08/786-4862 from 9:00 to 11:00 to confirm tour times, www.riksdagen.se.

▲Museum of Medieval Stockholm (Medeltidsmuseet)

This modern, well-presented museum offers a look at medieval Stockholm. When the government was digging a parking garage near the parliament building in the 1970s, workers uncovered a major archaeological find: parts of the town wall that King Gustav Vasa built in the 1530s, as well as a churchyard. This underground museum preserves these discoveries and explains how Stockholm grew from a medieval village to a major city, with a focus on its interactions with fellow Hanseatic League trading cities. Lots of artifacts, models, life-size dioramas, and sound and lighting effects—all displayed in a vast subterranean space—help bring the story to life.

The museum does a particularly good job of profiling individuals who lived in medieval Stockholm; their personal stories vividly set the context of the history. You'll also see the preserved remains of a small cannon-ship from the 1520s and a reconstructed main market square from 13th-century Stockholm.

Cost and Hours: Free, Tue-Sun 12:00-17:00, Wed until 19:00, closed Mon; free English guided tours July-Aug Tue-Sun at 14:00, audioguide-20 SEK, enter museum from park in front of parliament—down below as you cross the bridge, tel. 08/5083-1790, www.medeltidsmuseet.stockholm.se.

Nearby: The museum sits in **Strömparterren** park. With its café and Carl Milles statue of the *Sun Singer* greeting the day, it's a pleasant place for a sightseeing break (pay WC in park, free WC in museum).

Riddarholmen
Literally the "Knights Isle," Riddarholmen is the quiet and stately far side of Gamla Stan, with a historic church, private palaces, and a famous view. The knights referred to in its name were the nobles who built their palaces on this little island to be near the Royal Palace, just across the way. The island, cut off from the rest of Gamla Stan by a noisy highway, is pretty lifeless, with impersonal government agencies filling its old mansions. Still, a visit is worthwhile for a peek at its church and to enjoy the famous view of City Hall and Lake Mälaren from its far end.

A statue of Birger Jarl (considered the man who founded Stockholm in 1252) marks the main square. Surrounding it are 17th-century private palaces of old noble families (now government buildings). And towering high above is the spire of the Riddarholmen Church. Established in the 13th century as a Franciscan church, this has been the burial place of nearly every Swedish royal since the early 1600s. If you're looking for a Swedish Westminster Abbey, this is it (50 SEK, daily 10:00-17:00, Oct-Nov until 16:00). An inviting, shady café at the far end of the island is where people (and photographers) gather for Riddarholmen's iconic Stockholm view.

DOWNTOWN STOCKHOLM
I've organized these sights and activities in the urban core of Stockholm by island and/or neighborhood.

On Kungsholmen, West of Norrmalm
▲▲City Hall (Stadshuset)
The Stadshuset is an impressive mix of eight million red bricks, 19 million chips of gilt mosaic, and lots of Stockholm pride. While churches dominate cities in southern Europe, in Scandinavian capitals, City Halls seem to be the most impressive buildings, celebrating humanism and the ideal of people working together in community. Built in 1923, this is still a functioning City Hall. The members of the city council—101 men and women representing the 850,000 citizens of Stockholm—are hobby legislators with

regular day jobs. That's why they meet in the evening once a week. One of Europe's finest public buildings, the site of the annual Nobel Prize banquet, and a favorite spot for weddings (they do two per hour on Saturday afternoons, when some parts of the complex may be closed), City Hall is particularly enjoyable and worthwhile for its entertaining and required 50-minute tour.

Cost and Hours: 110 SEK; English tours offered daily, generally June-Aug every 30 minutes 9:30-15:30, fewer off-season; schedule can change due to special events—call to confirm; 300 yards behind the central train station—about a 15-minute walk from either the station or Gamla Stan, bus #3 or #50, cafeteria open to public at lunch Mon-Fri; tel. 08/5082-9058, www.stockholm.se/stadshuset.

Visiting City Hall: On the tour, you'll see the building's sumptuous National Romantic-style interior (similar to Britain's Arts and Crafts style), celebrating Swedish architecture and craftwork, and created almost entirely with Swedish materials. Highlights include the so-called Blue Hall (the Italian piazza-inspired, brick-lined courtyard that was originally intended to be painted blue—hence the name—where the 1,300-plate Nobel banquet takes place); the City Council Chamber (with a gorgeously painted wood-beamed ceiling that resembles a Viking longhouse—or maybe an overturned Viking boat); the Gallery of the Prince (lined with frescoes executed by Prince Eugene of Sweden); and the glittering, gilded, Neo-Byzantine-style (and aptly named) Golden Hall, where the Nobel recipients cut a rug after the banquet.

In this over-the-top space, a glimmering mosaic Queen of Lake Mälaren oversees the proceedings with a welcoming but watchful

eye, as East (see Istanbul's Hagia Sophia and the elephant, on the right) and West (notice the Eiffel Tower, Statue of Liberty, and skyscrapers with the American flag, on the left) meet here in Stockholm. Above the door across the hall is Sweden's patron saint, Erik, who seems to have lost his head (due to some sloppy mosaic planning). On the tour, you'll find out exactly how many centimeters each Nobel banquet attendee gets at the table, why the building's plans were altered at the last minute to make the tower exactly one meter taller, where the prince got the inspiration for his scenic frescoes, and how the Swedes reacted when they first saw that Golden Hall (hint: they weren't pleased).

▲City Hall Tower

This 348-foot-tall tower rewards those who make the climb with the classic Stockholm view: The old church spires on the atmo-spheric islands of Gamla Stan pose together, with the rest of the green and watery city spread-eagle around them.

Cost and Hours: 50 SEK, daily 9:15-17:15, May and Sept until 15:55, closed Oct-April.

Crowd-Beating Tips: Only 30 people at a time are allowed up into the tower, every 40 minutes through-out the day. To ascend, you'll need a timed-entry ticket, available only in person at the tower ticket office on the same day. It can be a long wait for the next available time, and tickets can sell out by mid-afternoon. If you're touring City Hall, come to the tower ticket window first to see when space is available. Ideally an appointment will coincide with the end of your tour.

Visiting the Tower: A total of 365 steps lead to the top of the tower, but you can ride an elevator partway up—leaving you only 159 easy steps to the top.

First you'll climb up through the brick structure, emerging at an atmospheric hall filled with models of busts and statues that adorn City Hall and a huge, 25-foot-tall statue of St. Erik. The patron saint of Stockholm, Erik was supposed to be hoisted by cranes up through the middle of the tower to stand at its top. But plans changed, big Erik is forever parked halfway up the structure, and the tower's top is open for visitors to gather and enjoy the view.

From Erik, you'll twist gradually up ramps and a few steps at a time through the narrow, labyrinthine brick halls with peek-a-boo views of the city. Finally you'll emerge into the wooden section of the tower, where a spiral staircase brings you up to the roof terrace. Enjoy the view from there, but also take some time to look around at the building's features. Smaller statues of Erik, Klara, Maria Magdalena, and Nikolaus, all patron saints, face their respective parishes. Look up: You're in the company of the tower's nine bells. And if you listen carefully, you might hear departure-hall announcements wafting all the way up from the central train station.

▲National Museum of Fine Arts (Nationalmuseum)

Though mediocre by European standards, this 200-year-old museum is small, central, and user-friendly. An extensive renovation may cause it to be closed when you visit—check ahead. Highlights

include several canvases by
Rembrandt and Rubens, a fine
group of Impressionist works,
and a sizeable collection of
Russian icons. Seek out the ex-
quisite paintings by the Swedish artists Anders Zorn, Ernst
Josephson, and Carl Larsson.
An excellent audioguide de-
scribes the top works.

Cost and Hours: 100 SEK, can be more with special exhibits,
audioguide-30 SEK; museum may be closed for renovation, confirm times on website; likely Wed-Sun 11:00-17:00, until later Tue
and Thu, closed Mon; Södra Blasieholmshamnen, T-bana: Kungsträdgården, tel. 08/5195-4310, www.nationalmuseum.se.

Museum Highlights: The Stockholm-born **Carl Larsson**
(1853-1919) became very popular as the Swedish Norman Rock-
well, chronicling the everyday family life of his own wife and brood
of kids. His two vast, 900-square-foot murals celebrate Swedish
history and are worth a close look. *The Return of the King* shows
Gustav Vasa astride a white horse. After escaping the Stockholm
Bloodbath and leading Sweden's revolt, he drove out the Danes
and was elected Sweden's first king (1523). Now he marches his
victorious troops across a drawbridge, as Stockholm's burghers bow
and welcome him home. In *The Midwinter Sacrifice*, it's solstice eve,
and Vikings are gathered at the pagan temple at Gamla Uppsala.
Musicians blow the *lur* horns, a priest in white raises the ceremonial hammer of Thor, and another priest in red (with his back to
us) holds a sacrificial knife. The Viking king arrives on his golden
sled, rises from his throne, strips naked, gazes to the heavens, and
prepares to sacrifice himself to the gods of winter, so that spring
will return to feed his starving people.

The museum also dedicates space to **design,** spanning the
1500s up to present day. Of the more recent examples, the collection includes gracefully engraved glass from the 1920s, works from
the Stockholm Exhibition of 1930, industrial design of the 1940s,
Scandinavian Design movement of the 1950s, plastic chairs from
the 1960s, modern furniture from the 1980s, and the Swedish new
simplicity from the 1990s.

On Blasieholmen and Skeppsholmen

The peninsula of Blasieholmen pokes out from downtown Stockholm, and is tethered to the island of Skeppsholmen by a narrow bridge (with great views and adorned with glittering golden
crowns). While not connected to the city by T-bana or tram, you can
reach this area on bus #65 or the harbor shuttle ferry. Skeppshol-

men offers a peaceful break from the bustling city, with glorious views of Gamla Stan on one side and Djurgården on the other.

Museum of Modern Art (Moderna Museet)

This bright, cheery gallery on Skeppsholmen island is as far out as can be. For serious art lovers, it warrants ▲▲. The impressive per-

manent collection includes modernist all-stars such as Picasso, Braque, Dalí, Matisse, Munch, Kokoschka, and Dix; lots of goofy Dada art (including a copy of Duchamp's urinal); Pollock, Twombly, Bacon, and other postmodernists; and plenty of excellent contemporary stuff as well (don't miss the beloved Rauschenberg *Goat with Tire*). Swedish artists of the 20th and 21st centuries are also featured. The curators draw from this substantial well of masterpieces to assemble changing exhibits.

The museum's fine collection of modern and contemporary sculpture is installed on the leafy grounds of Skeppsholmen island—perfect for a stroll even when the museum is closed. The building also houses the Architecture and Design Center, with changing exhibits (www.arkdes.se).

Cost and Hours: Free but sometimes a fee for special exhibits; download the excellent, free audioguide to enhance your visit; open Tue and Fri 10:00-20:00, Wed-Thu and Sat-Sun until 18:00, closed Mon; fine bookstore, good shop, and harborview café; T-bana: Kungsträdgården plus 10-minute walk, or take bus #65; tel. 08/5202-3500, www.modernamuseet.se.

Östermalm

What this ritzy residential area lacks in museums or sights, it makes up for in posh style. Explore its stately streets, dine in its destination restaurants, and be sure to explore the delightful, upscale Saluhall food market right on Östermalmstorg (see "Eating in Stockholm," later). Östermalm's harborfront is hemmed in by the pleasant park called Nybroplan; from here, ferries lead to various parts of the city and beyond (as this is the jumping-off point for cruises into Stockholm's archipelago). If connecting to the sights in Djurgården, consider doing Östermalm by foot.

▲▲Swedish History Museum (Historiska Museet)

The displays and artifacts in this excellent museum cover all of Swedish history, but the highlights are its fascinating Viking exhibit and impressive Gold Room. Also worth a look are sections on Scandinavian prehistory, medieval church art, and a well-realized

Stockholm's Best Views

For a bird's-eye perspective on this wonderful urban mix of water, parks, concrete, and people, consider these viewpoints.

City Hall Tower: Top of the tower comes with the classic city view (see listing earlier).

Katarina: This viewing platform—offering fine views over the steeples of Gamla Stan—rises up from Slussen (the busy transit zone between Gamla Stan and Södermalm). The elevator making this an easy destination may be under renovation during your visit, in which case, you'll have to huff your way up. You can get to the platform via pedestrian bridge from Mosebacke Torg, up above in Södermalm. In good summer weather, you'll have to wade through the swanky tables of Eriks restaurant to reach the (free and public) viewpoint.

Himlen: Rising above Södermalm's main drag, the Skrapan skyscraper has a free elevator to the 25th-floor restaurant, called Himlen. While they're hoping you'll buy a meal (200-SEK starters, 350-SEK main courses) or nurse a 150-SEK cocktail in the lounge, it's generally fine to take a discreet peek at the 360-degree views—just march in the door at #78 and ride the elevator up to 25 (daily 14:00-late, Götgatan 78, tel. 08/660-6068, www.restauranghimlen.se).

Kaknäs Tower: This bold, concrete, 500-foot-tall TV tower—looming above the eastern part of the city, and visible from just about everywhere—

was once the tallest building in Scandinavia (55 SEK, Mon-Sat 9:00-22:00, Sun until 19:00, shorter hours off-season, restaurant on 28th floor, east of downtown—bus #69 from Nybroplan or Sergels Torg to Kaknästornet Södra stop, tel. 08/667-2105, www.kaknastornet.se).

display about the Danish invasion of 1361—the battle of Gotland—in which 1,800 ill-equipped Swedish farmers lost their lives.

Cost and Hours: Free, daily 10:00-17:00; Sept-May closed Mon and open Wed until 20:00; a few blocks north of the Djurgården bridge at Narvavägen 13, bus #67 stops out front, tel. 08/5195-5562, www.historiska.se.

STOCKHOLM

Tours: Audioguide-30 SEK. Daily guided tours are offered in summer (at 12:00 and 13:00), and kids' activities are available in an inner courtyard until 16:00.

Visiting the Museum: The featured exhibit (on the ground floor), titled simply **"Vikings,"** probes the many stories and myths about these people. Were they peaceful traders and farmers—or brutal robbers and pillagers? The focus is on everyday activities, religious beliefs, and family life in the years from 800 to 1050—the Viking Age.

A reconstruction of a Viking village gives a view of early trading communities, but most people lived by farming, hunting, and fishing. Exhibits feature grave goods, combs of horn and bone, gaming pieces, and brooches. A rare find is a wooden chest filled with tools and scrap metal, believed to have belonged to a blacksmith/carpenter.

A fine section of "picture stones" relate the stories of the Norse gods, and amulets shaped like little hammers demonstrate the importance of the god Thor. The small group of Vikings who did venture abroad to trade (and to pillage) returned to Scandinavia with new customs—including Christianity.

The **"Gold Room"** (in the basement) dazzles viewers with about 115 pounds of gold: spiral hair ornaments from 1500 B.C.; gold collars worn by fifth-century aristocrats; hoards of coins from Roman and Arab empires; once-buried treasure troves of jewelry and votive objects; and medieval jewel-encrusted reliquaries.

In all, the museum has about 3,000 finely crafted gold objects—largely thanks to Swedish legislation that has protected antiquities since the 17th century.

Waterside Walk

Enjoy Stockholm's ever-expanding shoreline promenades. Tracing the downtown shoreline while dodging in-line skaters and ice-cream trolleys (rather than cars and buses), you can walk from Slussen across Gamla Stan, all the way to the good ship *Vasa* in Djurgården. Perhaps the best stretch is along the waterfront Strandvägen street (from Nybroplan past weather-beaten old boats and fancy facades to Djurgården). As you stroll, keep in mind that there's free fishing in central Stockholm, and the harbor waters are restocked every spring with thousands of new fish. Locals tell of one lucky lad who pulled in an 80-pound salmon. The waterside lanes are extremely bike-friendly here and throughout Stockholm.

DJURGÅRDEN

Four hundred years ago, Djurgården was the king's hunting ground (the name means "Animal Garden"). You'll see the royal gate to the island immediately after the bridge that connects it to the main-

Stockholm's Djurgården

land. Now this entire lush island is Stockholm's fun center, protected as a national park. It still has a smattering of animal life among its biking paths, picnicking families, art galleries, various amusements, and museums, which are some of the best in Scandinavia.

Orientation: Of the three great sights on the island, the Vasa and Nordic museums are neighbors, and Skansen is a 10-minute walk away (or hop on any bus or tram—they come every couple of minutes). Several lesser or special-interest attractions (from the ABBA museum to an amusement park) are also nearby.

To get around more easily, consider **renting a bike** as you enter the island. You can get one at Sjöcaféet, a café just over the Djurgårdsbron bridge; they also rent boats (bikes-80 SEK/hour, 275 SEK/day; canoes-150 SEK/hour, kayaks-125 SEK/hour; open daily 9:00-21:00, closed off-season and in bad weather; handy city cycle maps, tel. 08/660-5757, www.sjocafeet.se).

In the concrete building upstairs from the café, you'll find a **Djurgården visitors center,** with free maps, island bike routes, brochures, and information about the day's events (daily in summer 8:00-20:00, shorter hours off-season).

Getting There: Take tram #7 from Sergels Torg (the stop is right under the highway overpass) or Nybroplan (in front of the gilded theater building) and get off at one of these stops: Nordic Museum (use also for Vasa Museum), Liljevalc Gröna Lund (for ABBA museum), or Skansen. In summer, you can take a city ferry from the southeast end of Gamla Stan or from Nybroplan (see "Getting Around Stockholm," earlier). Walkers enjoy the harborside Strandvägen promenade, which leads from Nybroplan directly to the island (described under "Waterside Walk," earlier).

Major Museums on Djurgården
▲▲▲Skansen

Founded in 1891, Skansen was the first in what became a Europe-wide movement to preserve traditional architecture in open-air

museums. It's a huge park gathering more than 150 historic buildings (homes, churches, shops, and schoolhouses) transplanted from all corners of Sweden. Other languages have borrowed the Swedish term "Skansen" (which originally meant "the Fort") to describe an "open-air museum." Today, tourists enjoy exploring this Swedish-culture-on-a-lazy-Susan, seeing folk crafts in action and wonderfully furnished old interiors. Kids love Skansen, where they can ride a life-size wooden *Dala*-horse and stare down a hedgehog, visit Lill-Skansen (a children's zoo), and take a mini-train or pony ride. This is an enjoyable place to visit on summer days, when it's lively with families and tourists.

Cost and Hours: 180 SEK, kids-60 SEK, less off-season; park opens daily at 10:00, closes at 22:00 late June-Aug and progressively earlier the rest of the year; historical buildings generally open 11:00-17:00, late June-Aug some until 19:00, most closed in winter. Check their excellent online calendar for what's happening during your visit (www.skansen.se) or call 08/442-8000.

Music: Skansen does great music in summer. There's fiddling, folk dancing, and public dancing to live bands on Friday and Saturday nights. Confirm performance times before you go.

Visiting Skansen: Skansen isn't designed as a one-way loop; it's a sprawling network of lanes and buildings, yours to explore. For the full story, invest in the museum guidebook (sold at the info booth just after the entrance). With the book, you'll understand each building you duck into and even learn about the Nordic animals awaiting you in the zoo. While you're at the info booth, check the live crafts schedule to make a smart Skansen plan (the scale model displayed at the entrance will give you an idea of the park's size—and the need for a plan). Guides throughout the park are happy to answer your questions—but only if you ask them. The old houses come alive when you take the initiative to get information.

From the entrance, go up the stairs and bear left to find the escalator, and ride it up to **"The Town Quarter"** (Stadskvarteren), where shoemakers, potters, and glassblowers are busy doing their traditional thing (daily 10:00-17:00) in a re-created Old World Stockholm. Continuing deeper into the park—past the bakery, spice shop/grocery, hardware store, and a cute little courtyard café—you'll reach the central square, **Bollnästorget** (signed as "Central Skansen" but

labeled on English maps as "Market Street"), with handy food stands. The rest of Sweden spreads out from here. Northern Swedish culture and architecture is in the north (top of park map), and southern Sweden's in the south (bottom of map). Various homesteads—each clustered protectively around an inner courtyard—are scattered around the complex.

Poke around. Follow signs—or your instincts. It's worth stepping into the old, red-wood Seglora Church (just past Bollnästorget), which aches with atmosphere under painted beams. The park has two zoos: Lill-Skansen is a children's petting zoo. Beyond the big brick spa tower and carnival rides sprawls the Scandinavian Animals section, with bears, wolves, moose ("elk"), seals, reindeer (near the Sami camp), and other animals.

Eating at Skansen: The park has ample eating options to suit every budget. The most memorable—and affordable—meals are at the small folk food court on the main square, **Bollnästorget.** Here, among the duck-filled lakes, frolicking families, and peacenik local toddlers who don't bump on the bumper cars, kiosks dish up "Sami slow food" (smoked reindeer), waffles, hot dogs, and more. There are lots of picnic benches—Skansen encourages **picnicking.** (A small grocery store is tucked away across the street and a bit to the left of the main entrance.)

For a sit-down meal, the old-time **$$$ Stora Gungan Krog,** right at the top of the escalator in the craftsmen's quarter, is a cozy inn (indoor or outdoor lunches—meat, fish, or veggie—with a salad-and-cracker bar). Another snug spot is **$$ Gubbhyllan,** on the ground floor and fine porch of an old house (at base of escalator, just past main entrance). For a less atmospheric choice, consider one of three restaurants that share a modern building facing the grandstand (just up the hill inside the main entrance), all with nice views over the city: the simple **$$$ Skansen Terrassen** cafeteria; **$$$ Tre Byttor Taverne,** with 18th-century pub ambience; and, upstairs, the fussy **$$$$ Solliden** restaurant, with a dated blue-and-white dining hall facing a wall of windows; the main reason to eat here is the big *smörgåsbord* lunch (served 12:00-16:00).

Aquarium: The "aquarium"—featuring lemurs, meerkats, baboons, Gila monsters, giant anacondas, rattlesnakes, geckos, crocodiles, colorful tree frogs, and small sharks...but almost no fish—is located within Skansen, but is not covered by your Skansen ticket. Only animal lovers find it worth the steep admission price (120 SEK, July-Aug daily 10:00-19:00, closes earlier rest of year, tel. 08/660-1082, www.skansen-akvariet.se).

▲▲▲Vasa Museum (Vasamuseet)

Stockholm turned a titanic flop into one of Europe's great sightseeing attractions. The glamorous but unseaworthy warship *Vasa*—

top-heavy with an extra cannon deck—sank 40 minutes into her 1628 maiden voyage when a breeze caught the sails and blew her over. After 333 years at the bottom of Stockholm's harbor, she rose again from the deep with the help of marine archaeologists. Rediscovered in 1956 and raised in 1961, this Edsel of the sea is today the best-preserved ship of its age anywhere—housed since 1990 in a brilliant museum. The masts perched atop the roof—best seen from a distance—show the actual height of the ship.

Cost and Hours: 130 SEK, includes film and tour; daily 8:30-18:00; Sept-May 10:00-17:00 except Wed until 20:00; WCs on level 3, good café, Galärvarvet, Djurgården, tel. 08/5195-5810, www.vasamuseet.se.

Getting There: The *Vasa* is on the waterfront immediately behind the stately brick Nordic Museum (facing the museum,

walk around to the right) and a 10-minute walk from Skansen. From downtown, take tram #7.

Crowd-Beating Tips: There are two lines for tickets: on the right, for machines that take PIN-enabled credit cards; and on the left, for other cards or cash. The museum can have very long lines, but they generally move quickly—you likely won't wait more than 15-20 minutes.

If crowds are a concern, get here either right when it opens, or after about 16:00 (but note that the last tour starts at 16:30).

Tours: The free 25-minute **tour** is worthwhile. Because each guide is given license to cover whatever he or she likes, no two tours are alike—if you're fascinated by the place, consider taking two different tours to pick up new details. In summer, English tours run on the hour and half-hour (last tour at 16:30); off-season (Sept-May) tours go 3/day Mon-Fri, hourly Sat-Sun (last tour at 15:30). Listen for the loudspeaker announcement, or check at the info desk for the next tour. Alternatively, you can access the **audioguide** by logging onto the museum's Wi-Fi (www.vasamuseet.se/audioguide).

Film: The excellent 17-minute film digitally re-creates *Vasa*-era Stockholm (and the colorfully painted ship itself), dramatizes its sinking, and documents the modern-day excavation and preservation of the vessel. It generally runs three times per hour; virtually all showings are either in English or with English subtitles.

Visiting the Museum: For a thorough visit, plan on spending at least an hour and a half—watch the film, take a guided tour, and linger over the exhibits (this works in any order). After buying your ticket, head inside. Sort out your film and tour options at the information desk to your right.

Upon entry, you're prow-to-prow with the great ship. The *Vasa,* while not quite the biggest ship in the world when launched in 1628, had the most firepower, with two fearsome decks of cannons. The 500 carved wooden statues draping the ship—once painted in bright colors—are all symbolic of the king's power. The 10-foot lion on the magnificent prow is a reminder that Europe considered the Swedish King Gustavus Adolphus the "Lion from the North." With this great ship, Sweden was preparing to establish its empire and become more engaged in European power politics. Specifically, the Swedes (who already controlled much of today's Finland and Estonia) wanted to push south to dominate the whole of the Baltic Sea, in order to challenge their powerful rival, Poland.

Designed by a Dutch shipbuilder, the *Vasa* had 72 guns of the same size and type (a rarity on mix-and-match warships of the age), allowing maximum efficiency in reloading—since there was no need to keep track of different ammunition. Unfortunately, the king's unbending demands to build the ship high (172 feet tall) but skinny made it extremely unstable; no amount of ballast could weigh the ship down enough to prevent it from tipping.

Now explore the **exhibits,** which are situated on six levels around the grand hall, circling the ship itself. All displays are well described in English. You'll learn about the ship's rules (bread can't be older than eight years), why it sank (stale bread?), how it's preserved (the ship, not the bread), and so on. Best of all is the chance to do slow laps around the magnificent vessel at different levels. Now painstakingly restored, 98 percent of the *Vasa*'s wood is original (modern bits are the brighter and smoother planks).

On **level 4** (the entrance level), right next to the ship, you'll see a 1:10 scale model of the *Vasa* in its prime—vividly painted and fully rigged with sails. Farther along, models show how the *Vasa* was salvaged; a colorful children's section re-creates the time period; and a 10-minute multimedia show explains why the *Vasa* sank (alternating between English and Swedish showings). Heading behind the ship, you'll enjoy a great view of the sculpture-slathered stern of the *Vasa*. The facing wall features full-size replicas of the carvings, demonstrating how the ship was originally colorfully painted.

Several engaging displays are on **level 5.** "Life On Board" lets you walk through the gun deck and study cutaway models of the hive of activity that hummed below decks (handy, since you can't enter the actual ship). Artifacts—including fragments of clothing actually worn by the sailors—were salvaged along with the ship. "Battle!" is a small exhibit of cannons and an explanation of naval warfare.

Level 6 features "The Sailing Ship," with models demonstrating how the *Vasa* and similar vessels actually sailed. You'll see the (very scant) remains of some of the *Vasa*'s actual riggings and sails. **Level 7** gives you even higher views over the ship.

Don't miss **level 2**—all the way at the bottom (ride the handy industrial-size elevator)—with some of the most interesting exhibits. "The Ship" explains how this massive and majestic vessel was brought into being using wood from tranquil Swedish forests. Tucked under the ship's prow is a laboratory where today's scientists continue with their preservation efforts. The "Objects" exhibit shows off actual items found in the shipwreck, while "Face to Face" introduces you to some of those who perished when the *Vasa* sunk—with faces that were re-created from skeletal remains. Nearby, you'll see some of the skeletons found in the shipwreck. Those remains have been extensively analyzed, revealing remarkable details about the ages, diets, and general health of the victims.

As you exit, you'll pass a hall of (generally excellent) temporary exhibits.

▲Nordic Museum (Nordiska Museet)

Built to look like a Danish Renaissance palace, this museum offers a fascinating peek at 500 years of traditional Swedish lifestyles. The exhibits insightfully place everyday items into their social/

historical context in ways that help you really grasp various chapters of Sweden's past. It's arguably more informative than Skansen. Take time to let the excellent, included audioguide enliven the exhibits.

Cost and Hours: 120 SEK, free Wed Sept-May after 17:00; open daily 9:00-18:00, Sept-May 10:00-17:00 except Wed until 20:00; Djurgårdsvägen 6-16, at Djurgårdsbron, tram #7 from downtown, tel. 08/5195-4770, www.nordiskamuseet.se.

Visiting the Museum: Enter-ing the museum's main hall, you'll

STOCKHOLM

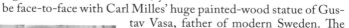

be face-to-face with Carl Milles' huge painted-wood statue of Gus-

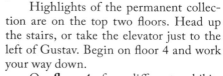

tav Vasa, father of modern Sweden. The rest of this floor is usually devoted to temporary exhibits.

Highlights of the permanent collection are on the top two floors. Head up the stairs, or take the elevator just to the left of Gustav. Begin on floor 4 and work your way down.

On **floor 4,** four different exhibits ring the grand atrium. The **"Homes and Interiors"** section displays 400 years of home furnishings, both as individual artifacts and as part of room dioramas. As you travel through this parade of furniture—from dark, heavily draped historical rooms to modern living rooms, and from rustic countryside cottages to aristocratic state bedrooms—you'll learn the subtle meaning behind everyday furniture that we take for granted. For example, the advent of television didn't just change entertainment—it gave people a reason to gather each evening in the living room, which, in turn, became a more-used (and less formal) part of people's homes. You'll learn about the Swedish designers who, in the 1930s, eschewed stiff-backed traditional chairs in favor of sleek perches that merged ergonomics and looks—giving birth to functionalism.

Also on this floor, the **"Folk Art"** section shows off colorfully painted furniture and wood carvings; vibrant traditional costumes; and rustic Bible-story illustrations that adorned the walls of peasants' homes. The **"Sápmi"** exhibit tells the fascinating and often overlooked story of the indigenous Sami people (formerly called "Lapps"), who lived in the northern reaches of Norway, Sweden,

Finland, and Russia centuries before Europeans created those modern nations. On display are shoes, ceremonial knives, colorful hats and clothing, and other features of Sami culture. You'll learn how their nomadic lifestyle—following their herds of grazing reindeer—allowed them to survive so far north, and how the Sami (who still number around 20,000) have had an impact on greater Swedish society. Finally, tucked behind the stairwell, the "Small Things" collection shows off timepieces, ceramics, and tobacco pipes, among other items.

Floor 3 has several smaller exhibits. The most interesting are **"Table Settings"** (with carefully set tables from the 16th century until about 1950, representing customs and traditions around gathering to share food and drink—from an elegant tea party to a rowdy pub) and **"Traditions"** (showing and describing each old-time celebration of the Swedish year—from Christmas to Midsummer—as well as funerals, confirmations, and other life events). Also on display: 300 years of Swedish attire (including a fun video showing how complicated and time-consuming it was for a woman to dress in the 18th century); jewelry and textile exhibits; a dollhouse and toy collection; and a photo exhibition pulled from the museum's archive.

▲ABBA: The Museum

The Swedish pop group ABBA was, for a time, a bigger business than Volvo. Since bursting on the scene in 1974 by winning the Eurovision Song Contest with "Waterloo," and serenading Sweden's newly minted queen with "Dancing Queen" in 1976, they've sold more than 380 million records, and the musical based on their many hits, *Mamma Mia!,* has been enjoyed by 50 million people. It was only a matter of time before Stockholm opened an ABBA museum, which is conveniently located just across the street from Skansen and next to Gröna Lund amusement park. Like everything ABBA, it is aggressively for-profit and slickly promoted, with the steepest ticket price in town. True to its subject, it's bombastic, glitzy, and highly interactive. If you like ABBA, it's lots of fun; if you love ABBA, it's ▲▲▲ nirvana.

Cost and Hours: 250 SEK—credit cards only, 595 SEK family ticket covers two adults and up to four kids; daily 9:00-19:00, Sept-May 10:00-18:00 except Wed until 19:00, Djurgårdsvägen 68, bus #44 or tram #7 to Liljevalc Gröna Lund stop, tel. 08/1213-2860, www.abbathemuseum.com.

Tours: ABBA aficionados will happily fork over 20 SEK extra for the intimate audioguide, in which Agnetha, Benny, Björn, and Anni-Frid share their memories, in their own words.

Getting In: Only 75 people are let in every 15 minutes with timed-entry tickets. The museum strongly encourages getting tickets in advance from their website or at the TI. In fact, they'll charge you 20 SEK extra per ticket to buy in person (but computer terminals are standing by if you want to "prebook" on the spot). It can be crowded on summer weekends, in which case you may have to wait for a later time.

Visiting the Museum: The museum is high-tech, with plenty of actual ABBA artifacts, re-creations of rooms where the group did its composing and recording (including their famous "Polar Studio" and their rustic archipelago cottage), a room full of gold and platinum records, plenty of high-waisted sequined pantsuits, and lots of high-energy video screens.

Included in the ticket is a "digital key" that lets you take advantage of several interactive stations. For example, you can record a music video karaoke-style as a fifth member of the group—with virtual ABBA members dancing around you—and share your musical debut via the museum's website. A small wing features the Swedish Music Hall of Fame, but apart from that, it's all ABBA.

Waterfront Sights

While the tram zips sightseers between the Vasa Museum and Skansen, it's a short, enjoyable, and very scenic walk along the waterfront—a delight on a nice day. You'll see food stands, boats bobbing in the harbor, and sunbathing Swedes.

You'll also pass several sights, listed here in the order you'll reach them (from the Djurgårdsbron bridge): **Junibacken** is a fairytale house based on the writings of Astrid Lindgren, who created *Pippi Longstocking*. While oriented toward Swedish kids, American children may enjoy it, too (www.junibacken.se). The pier directly in front of the Vasa Museum is actually part of the **Maritime Museum** (Sjöhistoriska), where historic ships are moored (typically big icebreakers from the Arctic, and sometimes military boats). About halfway along the waterfront is the **Museum of Spirits** (see next listing), offering a weird but welcome break from heavier sightseeing. Finally, you'll reach **Vikingaliv,** a small myth-busting museum about the Vikings that uses interactive displays to present them as colonizers and traders more than looters and warriors (you won't find a horned helmet in the place). A low-tech, hokey 10-minute ride tells "Ragnfrid's Saga" (the fictional story of the long-suffering wife of a voyaging husband; www.vikingaliv.se).

Museum of Spirits (Spiritmuseum)

The museum's highly conceptual permanent exhibit considers the role of alcohol—and specifically, flavored vodkas—in Swedish society. While Sweden got a reputation for its "loose morals" in the 1970s (mostly surrounding sex and nudity), at the same time it was extremely puritanical when it came to alcohol; the government actively tried to get Swedes to stop drinking (hence the liquor-store system and sky-high alcohol taxes that still exist). In the exhibit's season-themed rooms, you'll be able to smell different types of flavored liquors (orange in the spring, elderflower in the summer, and so on); upstairs, you can ace a virtual pub quiz, recline (or nap) in the boozy drunk-simulator room, and step into a garishly lit, buzzing room that simulates a hangover. The temporary exhibits here are also quite good.

Cost and Hours: 120 SEK, 250-SEK ticket adds a taster kit of flavored vodkas; Mon 10:00-17:00, Tue-Sat until 19:00, Sun 12:00-17:00, shorter hours off-season; summertime beer pier opens for dining and 17 types of draft beer, Djurgårdsvägen 38, tel. 08/1213-1300, www.spritmuseum.se.

Other Djurgården Sights
Gröna Lund Amusement Park
Stockholm's venerable and lowbrow Tivoli-type amusement park still packs in the local families and teens on cheap dates. It's a busy venue for local pop concerts.

Cost and Hours: 115 SEK to enter (free over 65 or under 7), then buy ride pass or coupons; daily late April-late Sept 12:00-23:00, closed off-season, www.gronalund.com.

▲Thielska Galleriet
If you liked the Larsson and Zorn art in the National Gallery, and/or if you're a Munch fan, this charming mansion on the water at the far end of the Djurgården park is worth the trip. The building was designed in the early 20th century for banker and art patron Ernest Thiel as a residence, but with skylight galleries to accommodate his extensive collection, which has hung here ever since.

Cost and Hours: 130 SEK, Tue-Sun 12:00-17:00, closed Mon, bus #69 (not #69K) from downtown, tel. 08/662-5884, www.thielska-galleriet.se.

▲Biking the Garden Island
In all of Stockholm, Djurgården is the most natural place to enjoy a bike ride. There's a good and reasonably priced bike-rental place just over the bridge as you enter the island (Sjöcaféet; see beginning of Djurgården section, earlier), and a world of parklike paths and lanes with harbor vistas to enjoy.

Ask for a free map and route tips when you rent your bike. Figure about an hour to pedal around Djurgården's waterfront perimeter; it's mostly flat, but with some short, steeper stretches that take you up and over the middle of the island. Those who venture beyond the Skansen park find themselves nearly all alone in the lush and evocative environs.

At the summit of the island you'll come upon Rosendal's Garden, with a bakery and café. You can sit in the greenhouse or in the delightful orchard or flower garden, where locals come to pick a bouquet and pay by the weight. (The garden is fertilized by the horse pies from adjacent Skansen.) Just beyond is the **Rosendals Slott,** the cute mini-palace of Karl Johans XIV, founder of the Bernadotte dynasty. This palace, in the so-called Karl Johans style ("Empire style"), went together in prefabricated sections in the 1820s. The story is told on a board in front, and a 9-ton porphyry vase graces the backyard.

A garden café at the eastern tip of the island offers a scenic break midway through your pedal. For a longer ride, you can cross the canal to the Ladugårdsgärdet peninsula ("Gärdet" for short), a swanky, wooded residential district just to the north.

SÖDERMALM

Just south of Gamla Stan, the Södermalm district is the real-life antidote to the upscale areas where most visitors spend their time. While it has few tourist sights (aside from the Fotografiska museum, and the Stockholm City Museum, which may be closed for renovation when you visit), Södermalm offers fine views and fun places to eat (for recommendations and more on this area, see "Södermalm Streets and Eats," later). Towering over Södermalm's main road is the Skrapan building, with the Himlen view terrace on its 25th floor (see "Stockholm's Best Views" sidebar, earlier).

▲Fotografiska (Photography Museum)

This museum, in a renovated 1906 industrial building right on the Stadsgården embankment, is fun and appealing. The focus is on contemporary and international photography, exhibited in well-curated, thematic displays that change several times a year. It's a complete destination, with a top-floor café giving drop-dead views over the city (open until 21:00 in summer), a people-watching terrace café on the embankment, and a browse-worthy store.

Cost and Hours: 135 SEK—credit cards only, daily 9:00-23:00, later on weekends, at Stadsgårdshamnen 22 (a 10-minute walk from Slussen; hop-on, hop-off boats stop here), tel. 08/5090-0500, www.fotografiska.eu.

ON THE OUTSKIRTS

The home and garden of Carl Milles, Sweden's greatest sculptor, is less than an hour from the city center. For sights farther outside

Stockholm (all reachable by public transportation), see the next chapter.

▲Millesgården

The villa and garden of Carl Milles is a veritable forest of statues by Sweden's greatest sculptor. Millesgården is dramatically situated on a bluff overlooking the harbor in Stockholm's upper-class suburb of Lidingö. While the art is engaging and enjoyable, even the curators have little to say about it from an interpretive point of view—so your visit is basically without guidance. But in Milles' house, which dates from the 1920s, you can see his north-lit studio and get a sense of his creative genius.

Carl Milles spent much of his career teaching at the Cranbrook Academy of Art in Michigan. But he's buried here at his villa, where he lived and worked for 20 years, lovingly designing this sculpture garden for the public. Milles wanted his art to be displayed on pedestals...to be seen "as if silhouettes against the sky." His subjects—often Greek mythological figures such as Pegasus or Poseidon—stand out as if the sky were a blank paper. Yet unlike silhouettes, Milles' images can be enjoyed from many angles. And Milles liked to enliven his sculptures by incorporating water features into his figures. *Hand of God,* perhaps his most famous work, gives insight into Milles' belief that when the artist created, he was—in a way—divinely inspired.

Cost and Hours: 150 SEK; daily 11:00-17:00 except closed Mon Oct-April; English booklet explains the art, restaurant and café, tel. 08/446-7590, www.millesgarden.se.

Getting There: Catch the T-bana to Ropsten, then take bus #207 to within a five-minute walk of the museum; several other #200-series buses get you close enough to walk (allow about 45 minutes total each way).

Shopping in Stockholm

Sweden offers a world of shopping temptations. Smaller stores are open weekdays 10:00-18:00, Saturdays until 17:00, and Sundays 11:00-16:00. Some of the bigger stores (such as NK, H&M, and Åhléns) are open later on Saturdays and Sundays.

Fun Chain Stores

These chains have multiple branches around town; the most convenient are marked on the "Stockholm Hotels & Restaurants" map.

DesignTorget, dedicated to contemporary Swedish design, receives a commission for selling the unique works of local designers (generally Mon-Fri 10:00-19:00, Sat until 18:00, Sun 11:00-17:00, big branch underneath Sergels Torg—enter from basement level of Kulturhuset, other branches are at Nybrogatan 23 and at the airport, www.designtorget.se).

Systembolaget is Sweden's state-run liquor store chain. A sample of each bottle of wine or liquor sits in a display case. A card in front explains how it tastes and suggests menu pairings. Look for the item number and order at the counter. Branches are in Hötorget underneath the movie theater complex, in Norrmalm at Vasagatan 21, and just up from Östermalmstorgat Nybrogatan 47 (Mon-Wed 10:00-18:00, Thu-Fri until 19:00, Sat until 15:00, closed Sun, www.systembolaget.se).

Gudrun Sjödén is named for its fashion-designer founder, whose life's work has been creating cheery, functional clothing for Swedish women. Some might sniff at her sensible but colorful designs (some inspired by her summer garden), but they're free-spirited in a Pippi Longstocking sort of way (think aubergine and sunflower). You'll love it or hate it—all around town (at Regeringsgatan 30, Götgatan 44, and Stora Nygatan 33, daily 10:00-19:00, Sat until 17:00, Sun 12:00-16:00, www.gudrunsjoden.com).

Hamngatan

The main shopping zone between Kungsträdgården and Sergels Torg (described in "Stockholm's Modern City Walk," earlier) has plenty of huge department stores. At the top of Kungsträdgården, **Illums Bolighus** is a Danish design shop. Across the street, **Nordiska Kompaniet** (NK) is elegant and stately; the Swedish design (downstairs) and kitchenware sections are particularly impressive. The classy **Gallerian** mall is just up the street from NK and stretches seductively nearly to Sergels Torg. The **Åhléns** store, kitty-corner across Sergels Torg, is less expensive than NK and has two cafeterias and a supermarket. Affordable clothing chain **H&M** has a store right across the street. Tucked behind Åhléns is **Kartbutiken,** a handy map-and-guidebook shop that covers all of Sweden, Scandinavia, and beyond (daily, at Mäster Samuelsgatan 54).

Mood Stockholm

The city's most exclusive mall is a downtown block filled with big-name Swedish and international designers, plus a pricey food court and restaurants. The upscale decor and mellow music give it a Beverly Hills vibe (Mon-Fri 10:00-20:00, Sat until 18:00, Sun 11:00-17:00, Regeringsgatan 48). The mall anchors a ritzy, pedestrianized shopping zone; for more exclusive shops, browse the nearby streets Jakobsbergsgatan and Biblioteksgatan.

Södermalm

When Swedes want the latest items by local designers, they skip the downtown malls and head for funky Södermalm. **Götgatan,** the main drag that leads from Slussen up to this neighborhood, is a particularly good choice, with shop after shop of mostly Swedish designers. Boutiques along here—some of them one-offs, others belonging to Swedish chains—include Weekday (known for denim), Filippa K (high-end attire), and Tiogruppen (colorful bags and fabrics). More intrepid shoppers will want to explore the area south of **Folkungagatan**—"SoFo," where scores of fun stores feature new and vintage clothing, housewares, and jewelry in the streets surrounding Nytorget.

Nybrogatan

This short and pleasant traffic-free street, which connects Östermalmstorg with the Nybroplan waterfront, is lined with small branches of interesting design shops, including Nordiska Galleriet (eye-catching modern furniture, at #11). It also has shoe and handbag stores, and an enticing cheese shop and bakery.

Flea Markets

For a *smörgåsbord* of Scanjunk, visit the **Loppmarknaden,** northern Europe's biggest flea market, at Vårberg Center (free entry weekdays and Sat-Sun after 15:00, 10-15 ISK on weekends—when it's busiest; Mon-Fri 11:00-18:00; Sat 10:30-16:00, Sun from 11:00; T-bana: Vårberg, tel. 08/710-0060, www.loppmarknaden. se). Hötorget, the produce market, also hosts a Sunday flea market in summer.

Nightlife and Entertainment in Stockholm

Bars and Music in Gamla Stan

The street called Stora Nygatan, with several lively bars, has perhaps the most accessible and reliable place for live jazz in town: Stampen. Several pubs here offer live Irish traditional music sessions or bluegrass several times each week; they tend to share musicians, who sometimes gather at one of these pubs for impromptu jam sessions (ask around, or stroll this street with your ears peeled). While it may seem odd to listen to Irish or bluegrass music in Stockholm, these venues are extremely popular with locals.

Stampen is two venues under one roof: a stone-vaulted cellar below (called Geronimo's FGT) and a fun-loving saloon-like jazz and R&B bar upstairs (check out the old instruments and antiques hanging from the ceiling). There's live music every night that Stampen is open (cover Fri-Sat only; Tue-Fri and Sun 17:00-late, Sat from 14:00, closed Mon, Stora Gråmunkegränd 7, tel. 08/205-793, www.stampen.se). Geronimo's, downstairs, is more of a nightclub/ concert venue with a menu inspired by the American Southwest (Tue-Sun 17:00 until late, enter at Stora Nygatan 5). For locations, see the "Gamla Stan Hotels & Restaurants" map.

Several other lively spots are within a couple of blocks of Stampen on Stora Nygatan. Your options include **Wirströms Pub** (live blues bands play in crowded cellar Mon-Sat 21:00-24:00, no cover; daily 11:00-late, Stora Nygatan 13, www.wirstromspub.se); **O'Connells Irish Pub** (a lively expat sports bar with music—usually Tue-Sat at 21:00; Mon-Sat 11:00-late, Sun from 12:00, Stora Nygatan 21, www.oconnells.se); and **The Liffey** (classic Irish pub with 150-180-SEK pub grub, live music Wed-Sun from 21:30; daily 12:00-late, Stora Nygatan 40-42, www.theliffey.se).

Icebar Stockholm

If you just want to put on a heavy coat and gloves and drink a fancy vodka in a modern-day igloo, consider the fun, if touristy, Icebar Stockholm. Everything's ice— shipped down from Sweden's far north. The bar, the glasses, even the tip jar are made of ice. You get your choice of vodka drinks and 45 minutes to enjoy the scene (online booking-199 SEK, drop-ins-210 SEK—on weekends drop-ins only allowed after 21:45, additional  drinks-95 SEK, reservations smart; daily 11:15-24:00, Sept-May from 15:00; in the Nordic C Hotel adjacent to the main train station's Arlanda Express platform at Vasaplan 4, tel. 08/5056-3520, www.icebarstockholm.se). If you go too early, it can be really dead—you'll be all alone. At busy times, people are let in all at once every 45 minutes. That means there's a long line for drinks, and the place goes from being very crowded to almost empty as people gradually melt away. While there are ice bars all over Europe now, this was the second one to open (after the Ice Hotel in Lapland). And it really is pretty cool...a steady 23°F.

Cinema

In Sweden, international movies are shown in their original language with Swedish subtitles. Swedish theaters sometimes charge more for longer films, and tickets come with assigned seats (drop by to choose seats and buy a ticket, box offices generally open 11:00-22:00 daily). The Hötorget and Drottninggatan neighborhoods have many theaters.

STOCKHOLM

Swedish Massage, Spa, and Sauna

To treat yourself to a Swedish spa experience—maybe with an authentic "Swedish massage"—head for the elegant circa-1900 **CentralBadet Spa.** It's along downtown's main strolling street, Drottninggatan, tucked back inside a tranquil and inviting garden courtyard. Admission includes entry to an extensive gym, "bubble-pool," sauna, steam room, "herbal/crystal sauna," and an elegant Art Nouveau pool. Most areas are mixed-gender, with men and women together, but some areas are reserved for women. If you won't make it to Finland, enjoy a sauna here. Bring your towel into the sauna—not for modesty, but for hygiene (to separate your body from the bench). The steam room is mixed; bring two towels (one for modesty and the other to sit on). The pool is more for floating than for jumping and splashing. The leafy courtyard restaurant is a relaxing place to enjoy affordable, healthy, and light meals (220 SEK, 320 SEK on Sat, towels and robes available for rent; slippers required—20 SEK to buy, 10 SEK to rent; Mon-Fri 7:00-20:30; Sat 8:00-19:30, Sun until 17:30; ages 18 and up, Drottninggatan 88, 10 minutes up from Sergels Torg, tel. 08/5452-1300, reservation tel. 08/218-821, www.centralbadet.se).

Sleeping in Stockholm

Between business travelers and the tourist trade, occupancy for Stockholm's hotels is healthy but unpredictable, and most hotels' rates vary from day to day with demand.

Consider hostels here—Stockholm's are among Europe's best, offering good beds in simple but interesting places. Each has helpful English-speaking staff, pleasant family rooms, and good facilities.

NEAR THE TRAIN STATION

$$$$ Freys Hotel is a Scan-mod, four-star place, with 127 compact, smartly designed rooms. It's well-situated for train travelers, located on a dead-end pedestrian street across from the central station. While big, it works hard to be friendly and welcoming. Its cool, candlelit breakfast room becomes a bar in the evening, popular for its selection of Belgian microbrews (air-con, Bryggargatan 12, tel. 08/5062-1300, www.freyshotels.com, freys@freyshotels.com).

$$$$ Scandic No. 53 injects modernity into a classic old building a few blocks from the station. The 274 rooms are small and functional (no desk or chair in standard rooms) but comfortable. Everything surrounds a stylish, glassy atrium boasting a lounge/

STOCKHOLM

Sleep Code

Hotels are classified based on the average price of a typical en suite double room with breakfast in high season.

$$$$	**Splurge:** Most rooms over 2,000 SEK
$$$	**Pricier:** 1,500-2,000 SEK
$$	**Moderate:** 1,000-1,500 SEK
$	**Budget:** 500-1,500 SEK
¢	**Hostel/Backpacker:** Under 500 SEK
RS%	**Rick Steves discount**

Unless otherwise noted, credit cards are accepted, and free Wi-Fi is available. Comparison-shop by checking prices at several hotels (on each hotel's own website, on a booking site, or by email). For the best deal, *always book directly with the hotel.* Ask for a discount if paying in cash; if the listing includes **RS%,** request a Rick Steves discount.

restaurant (live music until 24:00 most weekends), and a peaceful outdoor courtyard (air-con, elevator, Kungsgatan 53, tel. 08/5173-6500, www.scandichotels.com, no53@scandichotels.com).

$$ Queen's Hotel enjoys a great location at the quiet top end of Stockholm's main pedestrian shopping street (about a 10-minute walk from the train station, or 25 minutes from Gamla Stan). The 59 rooms are well worn, but they're generally spacious and have big windows—and it's reasonably priced. Rooms facing the courtyard are quieter (RS%—if booking online enter rate code "RICKS," elevator, Drottninggatan 71A, tel. 08/249-460, www.queenshotel.se, info@queenshotel.se).

$$ Hotel Bema, a bit farther from the center, is a humble place that rents 12 fine rooms for some of the best prices in town (breakfast served at nearby café, reception open Mon-Fri 8:30-17:00, Sat-Sun 9:00-15:00, bus #65 from station to Upplandsgatan 13—near the top of the Drottninggatan pedestrian street, or walk about 15 minutes from the train station—exit toward *Vasagatan* and head straight up that street, tel. 08/232-675, www.hotelbema.se, info@hotelbema.se).

¢ City Backpackers, with 140 beds a quarter-mile from the station, is youthful but classy (sheets extra, breakfast extra, pay laundry, tours, sauna; Upplandsgatan 2A, tel. 08/206-920, www.citybackpackers.se, info@citybackpackers.se).

¢ City Lodge Hostel, on a quiet side street just a block from the central station, has 68 beds, a convivial lounge, and a kitchen with free cooking staples (sheets and towels extra, breakfast extra, no curfew, Klara Norra Kyrkogata 15, tel. 08/226-630, www.citylodge.se, info@citylodge.se).

¢-$$ Generator Stockholm, a big and lively hostel, has 244

STOCKHOLM

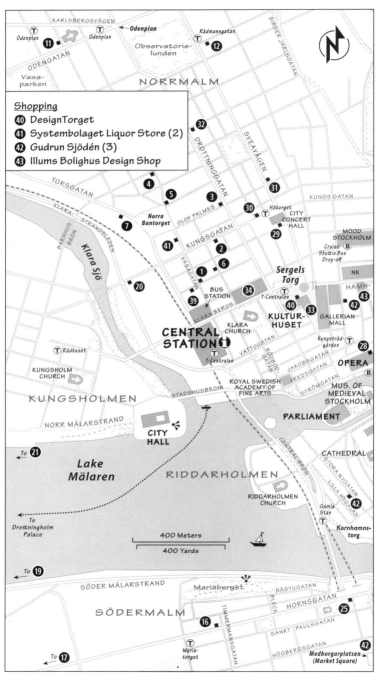

Shopping
40 DesignTorget
41 Systembolaget Liquor Store (2)
42 Gudrun Sjödén (3)
43 Illums Bolighus Design Shop

STOCKHOLM

Stockholm Hotels & Restaurants

Accommodations

1. Freys Hotel
2. Scandic No. 53
3. Queen's Hotel
4. Hotel Bema
5. City Backpackers
6. City Lodge Hostel
7. Generator Stockholm
8. Hotel Wellington
9. Story Hotel Stureplan
10. Hotel Riddargatan
11. Ibis Styles Stockholm Odenplan
12. Hostel Bed & Breakfast
13. Af Chapman Hostel
14. Skeppsholmen Hostel
15. NOFO Hotel/NOFO Loft
16. Hotel Hornsgatan
17. To Hotel Hellstens Malmgård
18. MS Birger Jarl Hotel
19. To Långholmen Hotel/Hostel

Eateries

20. Vapiano Pasta Pizza Bar (2)
21. To Mälarpaviljongen
22. To Södermalm & Skånegatan Eateries; Himlen Viewpoint
23. Mosebacke Beer Garden
24. Kvarnen Beer Hall
25. Akkurat Beer Hall
26. Veranda Restaurant
27. Restaurang B.A.R.
28. Bakfickan
29. Hötorgshallen, Kajsas Fisk & Systembolaget Liquor Store
30. Kungshallen Food Court
31. Urban Deli
32. Rolfs Kök
33. Cafeteria Panorama
34. Åhléns Dep't Store & Grocery
35. Saluhall
36. Restaurang Volt
37. Riche
38. Sushi Yama Express & DesignTorget
39. Icebar Stockholm

Scan-basic rooms spread across floors. The mix of dorms and private rooms all have private bathrooms. Close to the central station, it has a bar/café and restaurant on-site but no kitchen facilities (breakfast extra, family-friendly, elevator, bike rental, pay laundry; at Torsgatan 10, tel. 08/505-323, www.generatorhostels.com, stockholm@generatorhostels.com).

IN ÖSTERMALM

These options in Norrmalm and Östermalm are in stately, elegant neighborhoods of five- and six-story turn-of-the-century apartment buildings. All are within easy reach of downtown sights and close to T-bana, tram, or bus stops. Östermalm is an appealing part of town but without many hotels—it's also worth checking Airbnb for apartment rentals here.

$$$$ Hotel Wellington, two blocks off Östermalmstorg, is in a charming part of town and convenient to the harbor and Djurgården. It's modern and bright, with hardwood floors, 60 rooms, and a friendly welcome. While pricey, it's a cut above in comfort, and its great amenities—such as a very generous buffet breakfast, free coffee all day, and free buffet dinner—add up to a good value (RS%, free sauna, lobby bar, garden terrace, T-bana: Östermalmstorg, exit to Storgatan and walk past big church to Storgatan 6; tel. 08/667-0910, www.wellington.se, cc.wellington@choice.se).

$$$$ Story Hotel Stureplan is a colorful boutique hotel with a creative vibe. Conveniently located near a trendy dining zone between Östermalmstorg and the Nybroplan waterfront, it has 83 rooms above a sprawling, cleverly decorated, affordable restaurant. You'll book online, check yourself in at the kiosk, and receive a text message with your door key code (elevator, free minibar drinks, Riddargatan 6, tel. 08/5450-3940, www.storyhotels.com).

$$$ Hotel Riddargatan is well located on the edge of Östermalm—near the restaurants and shops on Nybrogatan and just two blocks from Nybroplan and the harbor. The front-desk staff is friendly, and the 78 rooms, while smallish, are nicely Scan-modern and perfectly functional. This is a hopping neighborhood: Ask for a quiet room when you book (elevator—but you'll climb a few steps to reception, bar/lounge, Riddargatan 14, tel. 08/5557-3000, www.profilhotels.se, hotelriddargatan@profilhotels.se).

$$$ Ibis Styles Stockholm Odenplan rents 76 cookie-cutter rooms on several floors of a late-19th-century apartment building (T-bana: Odenplan, Västmannagatan 61, reservation tel. 08/1209-0000, reception tel. 08/1209-0300, www.ibis.com, odenplan@uniquehotels.se).

¢-$ Hostel Bed and Breakfast is a tiny and easygoing independent hostel renting 36 beds in various dorm-style rooms.

Many families stay here (sheets and towels extra, laundry, across the street from T-bana: Rådmansgatan—use Stadsbibliotek exit, just off Sveavägen at Rehnsgatan 21, tel. 08/152-838, www.hostelbedandbreakfast.com, info@hostelbedandbreakfast.com).

IN GAMLA STAN

These options are in the midst of sightseeing, and a short bus or taxi ride from the train station. For locations, see the "Gamla Stan Hotels & Restaurants" map.

$$$$ Lady Hamilton Hotel, classic and romantic, is shoehorned into Gamla Stan on a quiet street a block below the cathedral and Royal Palace. The centuries-old building has 34 small but plush and colorfully decorated rooms. Each is named for a Swedish flower and is filled with antiques (elevator, Storkyrkobrinken 5, tel. 08/5064-0100, www.ladyhamiltonhotel.se, info@ladyhamiltonhotel.se).

$$$ Scandic Gamla Stan offers Old World elegance in the heart of Gamla Stan (a 5-minute walk from Gamla Stan T-bana station). Its 52 nicely decorated, smallish rooms have cheery wallpaper and hardwood floors (elevator, sauna, Nygatan 25, tel. 08/723-7250, www.scandichotels.com, gamlastan@scandichotels.com).

¢-$$ Castle House Inn is an Ikea-modern hostel/hotel situated in an ancient building that's located in an untrampled part of Gamla Stan, just a few steps off the harbor. The 53 whitewashed rooms are a mix of singles, mixed dorms, standard doubles, and family-friendly quads (breakfast extra, elevator, check-in 15:00-21:30, Brunnsgränd 4, tel. 08/551-5526, www.castlehouse.se, info@castlehouse.se).

ON SKEPPSHOLMEN

This relaxing island—while surrounded by Stockholm—feels a world apart, both in terms of its peacefulness and its somewhat less-convenient transportation connections (you'll rely on bus #65, the harbor shuttle ferry, or your feet—it's about a 20-minute walk from the train station). For locations, see the "Stockholm Hotels & Restaurants" map.

¢-$ Af Chapman Hostel, a permanently moored 100-year-old schooner, is Europe's most famous youth hostel and has provided a berth for the backpacking crowd for years. Renovated from keel to stern, the old salt offers 120 bunks in four- to six-bed rooms. Reception is at the Skeppsholmen Hostel (next, same contact info).

¢-$ Skeppsholmen Hostel is just ashore from the *Af Chapman* (private rooms, breakfast extra, 24-hour reception, tel. 08/463-2266, chapman@stfturist.se).

STOCKHOLM

ON OR NEAR SÖDERMALM

Södermalm is residential and hip, with Stockholm's best café and bar scene. You'll need to take the bus or T-bana to get here from the train station, making it less than convenient for those with limited time.

$$$ NOFO Hotel/$$ NOFO Loft is a hybrid hotel/hostel located in a 19th-century building that faces a big courtyard in the heart of Södermalm. The 48 luxe hotel rooms are decorated with individual flair; the 26 simple hostel rooms are under the eaves, with bathrooms down the hall (breakfast extra in hostel; T-bana: Medborgarplatsen or bus #53 from train station to Tjärhovsplan, then a 5-minute walk to Tjärhovsgatan 11; tel. 08/5031-1200, www.nofohotel.se, info@nofo.se).

$$$ Hotel Hornsgatan is a tidy, welcoming, nicely decorated B&B upstairs in an old townhouse facing a busy but elegant-feeling boulevard. Four of the 17 small rooms have private baths; the others share five modern bathrooms. Thoughtfully run by Clara and Scott, this is a good value for the location (elevator, reception staffed until 22:00—make arrangements if arriving late, Hornsgatan 66B, T-bana: Mariatorget plus a short walk, 15-minute walk from Slussen/Gamla Stan, tel. 08/658-2901, www.hotelhornsgatan.se, info@hotelhornsgatan.se).

$$$ Hotel Hellstens Malmgård is an eclectic collage of 50 rooms crammed with antiques in a circa-1770 mansion. No two rooms are alike, but all have modern baths and quirky touches such as porcelain stoves or four-poster beds. Unwind in its secluded cobblestone courtyard, and you may forget what century you're in (elevator, T-bana: Zinkensdamm, then a 5-minute walk to Brännkyrkagatan 110; tel. 08/4650-5800, www.hellstensmalmgard.se, hotel@hellstensmalmgard.se).

$ The MS Birger Jarl Hotel is a floating hotel with 130 cabins, varying from small simple rooms to superior cabins with private baths (family rooms, Wi-Fi in public spaces, on Stadsgårdskajen in Slussen, tel. 08/6841-0130, www.msbirgerjarl.se, family@msbirgerjarl.se).

¢-$$$$ Långholmen Hotel/Hostel is on Långholmen, a small island off Södermalm that was transformed in the 1980s from Stockholm's main prison into a lovely park. Rooms are converted cells in the old prison building. You can choose between **¢** hostel-style and **$$$$** hotel-standard rooms at many different price levels (sheets and breakfast extra in hostel; hotel rooms include breakfast; family rooms, laundry room, kitchen, cafeteria, free parking, swimming beach and jogging paths nearby; T-bana: Hornstull, walk 10 minutes down and cross small bridge to Långholmen island, then follow hotel signs 5 minutes farther; tel. 08/720-8500, www.langholmen.com, hotel@langholmen.com).

Eating in Stockholm

To save money, eat your main meal at lunch, when cafés and restaurants have daily specials called *dagens rätt* (generally Mon-Fri only). Most museums have handy cafés with lunch deals and often with fine views. Convenience stores stock surprisingly fresh takeaway food. As anywhere, department stores and malls are eager to feed shoppers and can be a good, efficient choice. If you want culturally appropriate fast food, stop by a local hot dog stand. Picnics are a great option—especially for dinner, when restaurant prices are highest. There are plenty of parklike, harborside spots to give your cheap picnic some class. I've also listed a few splurges—destination restaurants that offer a good sample of modern Swedish cooking.

IN GAMLA STAN

Most restaurants in Gamla Stan serve a weekday lunch special. Choose from Swedish, Asian, or Italian cuisine. Several popular

places are right on the main square (Stortorget) and near the cathedral. Järntorget, at the far end, is another fun tables-in-the-square scene. Touristy places line Västerlånggatan. You'll find more romantic spots hiding on side lanes, such as the stretch of Österlånggatan that hides below Köpmantorget square (where St. George is slaying the dragon). I've listed my favorites below (for locations, see "Gamla Stan Hotels & Restaurants" map).

$$ Grillska Huset is a cheap and handy cafeteria run by Stockholms Stadsmission, a charitable organization helping the poor. It's grandly situated right on the old square, with indoor and outdoor seating (tranquil garden up the stairs and out back), fine daily specials, a hearty salad bar, and a staff committed to helping others. You can feed the hungry (that's you) and help house the homeless at the same time (daily 10:00-21:00 except Sun-Mon until 20:00, Stortorget 3, tel. 08/787-8605). They also have a fine little bakery *(brödbutik)* with lots of tempting cakes and pastries (closed Sun).

$$$$ Kryp In, a small, cozy restaurant (the name means "hide away") tucked into a peaceful lane, has a stylish hardwood and candlelit interior, great sidewalk seating, and an open kitchen letting you in on Vladimir's artistry. If you dine well in Stockholm once (or twice), I'd do it here. It's gourmet without pretense. They serve delicious, modern Swedish cuisine with a 455-SEK three-course dinner. In the good-weather months, they serve weekend

STOCKHOLM

Restaurant Price Code

I've assigned each eatery a price category, based on the average cost of a typical main course. Drinks, desserts, and splurge items (steak and seafood) can raise the price considerably.

    $$$$ **Splurge:** Most main courses over 200 SEK
    $$$ **Pricier:** 150-200 SEK
    $$ **Moderate:** 100-150 SEK
    $ **Budget:** Under 100 SEK

In Sweden, a hot dog stand or other takeout spot is **$**; a sit-down café is **$$**; a casual but more upscale restaurant is **$$$**; and a swanky splurge is **$$$$**.

---

lunches, with specials starting at 120 SEK. Reserve ahead for dinner (275-290-SEK plates, daily 17:00-23:00, lunch Sat-Sun 12:00-16:00, a block off Stortorget at Prästgatan 17, tel. 08/208-841, www.restaurangkrypin.se).

$$ Vapiano Pasta Pizza Bar, a bright, high-energy, family-oriented eatery, issues you a smart card as you enter. Circulate to the different stations, ordering up whatever you like as they swipe your card. Portions are huge and easily splittable. As you leave, your card indicates the bill. Add flavor by picking a leaf of basil or rosemary from the potted plant on your table. Tables are often shared, making this a great place for solo travelers (daily 11:00-24:00, next to entrance to Gamla Stan T-bana station, Munkbrogatan 8, tel. 08/222-940). They also have locations on Östermalm (facing Humlegården park at Sturegatan 12) and Norrmalm (between the train station and Kungsholmen at Kungsbron 15)—for these locations, see the "Stockholm Hotels & Restaurants" map.

$$ Hermitage Restaurant is a faded, hippie-feeling joint that serves a decent vegetarian buffet in a communal dining setting (Mon-Fri 11:00-21:00, Sat-Sun from 12:00, Stora Nygatan 11, tel. 08/411-9500).

Picnic Supplies in Gamla Stan: The handy and affordable **Coop Nära** minimarket is strategically located on Järntorget, at the Slussen end of Gamla Stan; the **Munkbrohallen** supermarket downstairs in the Gamla Stan T-bana station is also very picnic-friendly (both long hours daily).

DINING ON THE WATER

In Gamla Stan: Sprawling along the harbor embankment, **$$$$ Mister French** faces a gorgeous Stockholm panorama—the main reason to eat here. The entire place opens up to the outdoors in good weather: Choose between the stylish bar (simple bar food), the full restaurant (French cuisine), or—my favorite—the lounge

STOCKHOLM

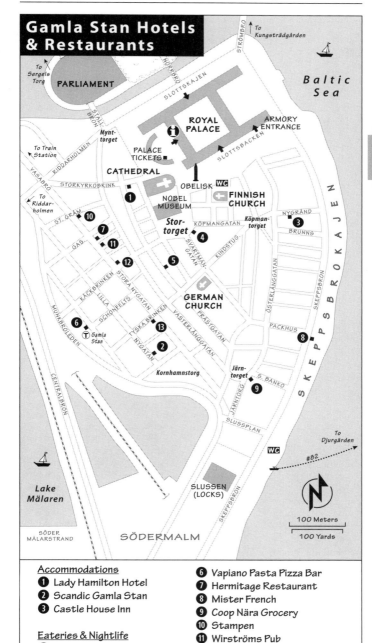

Gamla Stan Hotels & Restaurants

Accommodations
1. Lady Hamilton Hotel
2. Scandic Gamla Stan
3. Castle House Inn

Eateries & Nightlife
4. Grillska Huset
5. Kryp In
6. Vapiano Pasta Pizza Bar
7. Hermitage Restaurant
8. Mister French
9. Coop Nära Grocery
10. Stampen
11. Wirströms Pub
12. O'Connells Irish Pub
13. The Liffey Irish Pub

Swedish Cuisine

Most people don't travel to Sweden for the food. Though potatoes and heavy sauces are a focus of the country's cuisine, its variety of meat and fish dishes can be surprisingly satisfying. If you don't think you'll like Swedish or Scandinavian food, be sure to splurge at a good-quality place before you pass final judgment.

Every region of Sweden serves different specialties, but you'll always find *svenska köttbullar* on the menu (Swedish meatballs made from beef and pork in a creamy sauce). This Swedish favorite is topped with lingonberry jam, which is served with many meat dishes across Scandinavia. Potatoes, seemingly the only vegetable known to Sweden, make for hearty *kroppkakor* dumplings filled with onions and minced meat. The northern variation, *pitepalt,* is filled with pork. Southern Sweden takes credit for *pytt i panna,* a medley of leftover meat and diced potatoes that's fried and served with an egg yolk on top. And it seems that virtually every meal you'll eat here includes a side of boiled, small new potatoes.

Though your meals will never be short on starch, be sure to try Sweden's most popular baked good, *kanelbulle,* for a not-so-light snack during the day. This pastry resembles a cinnamon roll, but it's made with cardamom and topped with pearl sugar. Enjoy one during *fika,* the daily Swedish coffee break so institutionalized that many locals use the term as a verb (see the *"Fika"* sidebar, earlier).

Like those of its Nordic neighbors, Sweden's extensive coastline produces some of the best seafood in the world. A light, tasty appetizer is *gravad lax,* a dill-cured salmon on brown bread or crackers. You'll also likely encounter *Toast Skagen.* This appetizer-spread is made from shrimp, dill, mayonnaise, and Dijon mustard, and is eaten on buttered toast.

For a main course, the most popular seafood dish is crayfish. Though eaten only by the aristocracy in the 16th century, these shellfish have since become a nationwide delicacy; they're cooked in brine with dill and eaten cold as a finger food. Traditional crayfish parties take place outdoors on summer evenings, particularly in August. Friends and family gather around to indulge in this specialty with rye bread and a strong cheese. The Swedes also love Baltic herring; try *stekt strömming,* a specialty of the east coast, which is herring fried with butter and parsley. As usual, it's served with potatoes and lingonberry jam. Adventurous diners can have their herring pickled or fermented—or order more unusual dishes like reindeer.

As for beer, the Swedes classify theirs by alcohol content. The higher the number, the higher the alcohol content—and the price. *Klass 1* is light beer—very low-alcohol. *Klass 2* is stronger, but still mild. And *Klass 3* has the most body, the most alcohol, and the highest price.

with comfy sofas (daily 11:30-24:00, smart to reserve ahead in good weather, Tullhus 2, tel. 08/202-095, www.mrfrench.se).

In Kungsholmen, Behind City Hall: On a balmy summer's eve, **$$$ Mälarpaviljongen** is a dreamy spot with hundreds of locals enjoying the perfect lakefront scene, as twinkling glasses of rosé shine like convivial lanterns. From City Hall, walk 15 minutes along Lake Mälaren (a treat in itself) to find a hundred casual outdoor tables floating on pontoons and scattered among the trees on shore. When it's cool, they have heaters and blankets (open in good weather April-Sept daily 11:00-late, easy lakeside walk or T-bana to Fridhemsplan plus a 5-minute walk to Nörr Mälarstrand 63, no reservations, tel. 08/650-8701).

In Djurgården: Just over the Djurgårdsbron bridge, **$$-$$$ Sjöcaféet** is beautifully situated and greedily soaking up the afternoon sun, filling a woody terrace stretching along the harbor. In summer, this is a fine place for a meal or just a drink before or after your Skansen or *Vasa* visit. They have affordable lunch plates (Mon-Fri 11:00-13:00 only); after 14:00, you'll pay a bit more (order at the bar, daily 8:00-20:00, often later in summer, closed off-season, bike and boat rentals, tel. 08/661-4488). For the location of this and the next restaurant, see the "Stockholm's Djurgården" map.

$$$$ Oaxen Slip Bistro, a trendy harborfront place 200 yards below the main Skansen gate, serves creative Nordic cuisine with sturdy local ingredients in a sleek interior or on its delightfully woody terrace. Overlooking a canal in what feels like an old shipyard, and filled with in-the-know locals, this place is a real treat. Reservations are smart (daily 12:00-14:00 & 17:00-21:30, Beckholmsvägen 26, tel. 08/5515-3105, www.oaxen.com).

Dinner Cruises on Lake Mälaren: The big sightseeing company Strömma sells a variety of lunch and dinner cruises that allow you to enjoy the delightful waterways of Stockholm and the archipelago while you eat. Options include shorter dinner cruises to Drottningholm Palace (2.5 hours round-trip), longer ones to the outer archipelago (up to 5 hours), and *smörgåsbord* cruises around Lake Mälaren. For details and booking (and other options, including a shrimp cruise and a jazz cruise), check www.stromma.se.

SÖDERMALM STREETS AND EATS

This quickly gentrifying district, just south of Gamla Stan (steeply uphill from Slussen), has some of Stockholm's most enticing food options—especially for beer lovers. It's a bit less swanky, and therefore more affordable, than some of the city's more touristy neighborhoods. Combine dinner here with a stroll through a side of Stockholm many visitors miss. The most interesting areas to explore are along Götgatan and the zone south of Folkungagatan street—nicknamed "SoFo."

Götgatan and Medborgarplatsen

The neighborhood's liveliest street is Götgatan, which leads from Slussen steeply up into the heart of Södermalm. Here, mixed between the boutiques, you'll find cafés tempting you to join Swedish *fika* (coffee break), plus plenty of other eateries. Even if you don't dine in Södermalm, it's worth a stroll here just for the window-shopping fun.

At the top of the street, you'll pop out into the big square called Medborgarplatsen (you can also ride the T-bana right to this square). This neighborhood hangout is a great scene, with almost no tourists and lots of options—especially for Swedish fast food. Outdoor restaurant and café tables fill the square, which is fronted by a big food hall. The recommended Kvarnen beer hall is just around the corner (see later).

$$ Melanders Fisk, inside the Söderhallarna food hall, offers table service inside or takeaway from their deli counter—but come in good weather and you can enjoy your meal outside on the square. *Skagenröra*, shrimp with mayo on toast or filling a baked potato, is the signature dish—and dear to the Swedish heart. There's also a wine bar that stays open until 22:00 (food served Mon-Sat from 11:00 until at least 15:00, some nights as late as 20:00, Medborgarplatsen 3, tel. 08/644-4040).

Skånegatan and Nytorget

A bit farther south, these cross-streets make another good spot to browse among fun and enticing restaurants, particularly for ethnic cuisine.

$$$ Urban Deli Nytorget is half fancy artisanal delicatessen—with all manner of ingredients—and half white-subway-tile-trendy eatery, with indoor and outdoor tables filled with Stockholmers eating well. If it's busy—as it often is—they'll scrawl your name at the bottom of the long butcher-paper waiting list (no reservations). If it's full, you can grab a place at the bar and eat there—or shop in the attached upscale grocery (lots of creative boxed meals and salads to go) and picnic in the park across the street (daily 7:00-23:00, at the far end of Skånegatan at Nytorget 4, tel. 08/5990-9180). Another branch is near Hörtorget at Sveavägen 44 (see the "Stockholm Hotels & Restaurants" map).

$$$ Kohphangan, with an almost laughably over-the-top island atmosphere that belies its surprisingly good Thai food, has been a hit for 20 years. (Thailand is to Swedes what Mexico is to Americans—the sunny "south of the border" playground.) The ambience? Mix a shipwreck, Bob Marley, and a Christmas tree and you've got it (Mon-Fri 16:00-24:00, Sat-Sun from 12:00, Skå-negatan 57, tel. 08/642-5040).

$$ Gossip is a mellow, unpretentious hole-in-the-wall serving Bangladeshi street food (Mon-Fri 11:00-23:00, Sat-Sun from 13:00, Skånegatan 71, tel. 08/640-6901).

Beer and Pub Grub in Södermalm
Södermalm cultivates the most interesting beer scene in this beer-crazy city.

Beer Garden with a View: $$ Mosebacke, perched high above town, is a gravelly beer garden with a grand harbor view. The beer garden (open only on warm summer evenings) prides itself on its beer rather than its basic grub (read: bar snacks). It's a good place to mix with a relaxed young crowd. As each of the beer kiosks has its own specialties, survey all of them before making your choice (some open from 11:00, others later; a block inland from the top of the Katarina viewing platform, look for the triumphal arch at Mosebacke Torg 3, tel. 08/556-09890, www.sodrateatern.com). The adjacent restaurant serves fine **$$$$** plates.

Classic Swedish Beer Halls: Two different but equally traditional Södermalm beer halls serve well-executed, hearty Swedish grub in big, high-ceilinged, orange-tiled spaces with rustic wooden tables.

$$$ Kvarnen ("The Mill") is a reliable choice with a 1908 ambience. As it's the home bar for the supporters of a football club, it can be rough. Pick a classic Swedish dish from their fun and easy menu (Mon-Fri 11:00-late, Sat-Sun from 12:00, Tjärhovsgatan 4, tel. 08/643-0380).

$$$$ Pelikan, an old-school beer hall, is less sloppy and has nicer food, including meatballs as big as golf balls. It's a bit deeper into Södermalm (Mon-Thu 16:00-24:00, Fri-Sun from 12:00, Blekingegatan 40, tel. 08/5560-9290).

Trendier "Craft Beer" Pub: $$$ Akkurat has a staggering variety of microbrews—both Swedish and international (on tap and bottled)—as well as whisky. It's great if you wish you were in England with a bunch of Swedes (short pub-grub menu, daily 15:00-24:00 except Fri from 11:00 and Sun from 18:00, Hornsgatan 18, tel. 08/644-0015).

IN NORRMALM
At or near the Grand Hotel
$$$$ Royal Smörgåsbord: To stuff yourself with all the traditional Swedish specialties (a dozen kinds of herring, salmon, reindeer, meatballs, lingonberries, and shrimp, followed by a fine table of cheeses and desserts) with a super harbor view, consider splurging at the Grand Hotel's dressy **Veranda Restaurant.** While very tour-

isty, this is considered the finest *smörgåsbord* in town. The Grand Hotel, where royal guests and Nobel Prize winners stay, faces the harbor across from the palace. Pick up their English flier for a good explanation of the proper way to enjoy this grand buffet (and read about *smörgåsbords* in the Practicalities chapter). Reservations are often necessary (545 SEK in evening, less at lunch, drinks extra, open nightly 18:00-22:00, also open for lunch Sat-Sun 13:00-16:00 year-round and Mon-Fri 12:00-15:00 in May-Sept, no shorts after 18:00, Södra Blasieholmshamnen 8, tel. 08/679-3586, www.grandhotel.se).

$$$$ Restaurang B.A.R. has a noisy, fun energy, with diners surveying meat and fish at the ice-filled counter, talking things over with the chef, and then choosing a slab or filet. Prices are on the board, and everything's grilled (Mon-Fri 11:30-14:00 & 17:00 until late, Sat 16:00-late, closed Sun, behind the Grand Hotel at Blasieholmsgatan 4, tel. 08/611-5335). They also have a nice (short and lower-priced) takeaway menu.

At the Royal Opera House

The Operakällaren, one of Stockholm's most exclusive restaurants, runs a little "hip pocket" restaurant on the side called **$$$ Bakfickan,** specializing in traditional Swedish quality cooking at reasonable prices. It's ideal for someone eating out alone, or for anyone wanting an early dinner. Choose from two different daily specials or order from their regular menu. Sit inside—at tiny private side tables or at the big counter with the locals—or, in good weather, grab a table on the sidewalk, facing a cheery red church (Mon-Thu 11:30-22:00, Fri-Sat until 23:00, Sun 12:00-17:00, on the inland side of Royal Opera House, tel. 08/676-5809).

At or near Hötorget

Hötorget ("Hay Market"), a vibrant outdoor produce market just two blocks from Sergels Torg, is a fun place to picnic-shop. The outdoor market closes at 18:00, and many merchants put their unsold produce on the push list (earlier closing and more desperate merchants on Sat).

Hötorgshallen, next to Hötorget (in the basement under the modern cinema complex), is a colorful indoor food market with an old-fashioned bustle, plenty of exotic and ethnic edibles, and—in the tradition of food markets all over Europe—some great little eateries (Mon-Fri 10:00-18:00, Sat until 16:00, closed Sun). The best is **$$ Kajsas Fisk,** hiding behind the fish stalls. They serve delicious fish soup to little Olivers who can hardly believe they're getting...more. For 110 SEK, you get a big bowl of hearty soup, a simple salad, bread and crackers—plus one soup refill. Their *stekt strömming* (traditional fried herring and potato dish) is a favorite

(Mon-Thu 11:00-18:00, Fri until 19:00, Sat until 16:00, closed Sun, Hötorgshallen 3, tel. 08/207-262). There's a great kebab and falafel place a few stalls away.

$ Kungshallen, an 800-seat indoor food court across the square from Hötorget, has more than a dozen basic eateries. What it lacks in ambience it makes up for in variety, quick service, and generally lower prices. The main floor has sit-down places, while the basement is a shopping-mall-style array of fast-food counters, including Chinese, sushi, pizza, Greek, and Mexican (daily 11:00-22:00).

Just a few blocks away is a branch of **Urban Deli** (at Sveavägen 44), a good takeaway option described earlier under "Skånegatan and Nytorget."

On or near Drottninggatan

The pleasant, pedestrianized shopping street called Drottning-gatan, which runs from the train station area up into Stockholm's suburbs, is a fine place to find a forgettable meal but with memorable people-watching. Several interchangeable eateries with sidewalk tables line the street (and don't miss the delightful, leafy park courtyard of Centralbadet, at #88, with several outdoor cafés). None merits a special detour, except the next listing.

$$$$ Rolfs Kök, a vibrant neighborhood favorite, is worth the pleasant five-minute stroll up from the end of Drottninggatan. The long bar up front fades into an open kitchen hemmed in with happy diners at counters, and tight tables fill the rest of the space before spilling out onto the sidewalk. Trendy, casual, and inviting, this bistro features international fare with a focus on Swedish classics and a good wine list. Reservations are smart (Mon-Fri 11:30-24:00, Sat-Sun from 17:00, Tegnérgatan 41, tel. 08/101-696, www.rolfskok.se).

Near Sergels Torg

Kulturhuset: Handy for a simple meal with great city views, **$$ Cafeteria Panorama** offers cheap eats and a salad bar, inside and outside seating, and jaw-dropping vistas (90-SEK lunch specials with salad bar, Mon-Fri 11:00-19:00, Sat until 18:00, Sun until 17:00).

The many modern shopping malls and department stores around Sergels Torg all have appealing, if pricey, eateries catering to the needs of hungry local shoppers. **Åhléns** department store has a Hemköp supermarket in the basement (daily until 21:00) and two restaurants upstairs with 80-110-SEK daily lunch specials (Mon-Fri 11:00-19:30, Sat until 18:30, Sun until 17:30).

IN ÖSTERMALM

$$$ Saluhall, on Östermalmstorg (near recommended Hotel Wellington), is a great old-time indoor market dating from 1888. Depending on when you visit, the hall may be operating from an adjacent temporary market—or it may be completely refurbished, from top to bottom. Either way, you'll find top-quality artisanal producers and a variety of sit-down and takeout eateries. While it's nowhere near "cheap," it's one of the most pleasant market halls I've seen, oozing with upscale yet traditional Swedish class. Inside you'll find Middle Eastern fare, sushi, classic Scandinavian open-face sandwiches, seafood salads, healthy wraps, cheese counters, designer chocolates, gourmet coffee stands, and a pair of classic old sit-down eateries (Elmqvist and Tysta Mari). This is your chance to pull up a stool at a lunch counter next to well-heeled Swedes (Mon-Fri 9:30-19:00, Sat until 16:00, closed Sun).

$$$$ Restaurang Volt is a destination restaurant for those looking to splurge on "New Nordic" cooking: fresh, locally sourced ingredients fused into bold new recipes with fundamentally Swedish flavors. Owners Fredrik Johnsson and Peter Andersson fill their minimalist black dining room with just 31 seats, so reservations are essential (no a la carte, choose from 4- or 6-course tasting menus, Tue-Sat 18:00-24:00, closed Sun-Mon, Kommendörsgatan 16, tel. 08/662-3400, www.restaurangvolt.se).

$$$$ Riche, a Parisian-style brasserie just a few steps off Nybroplan at Östermalm's waterfront, is a high-energy place with a youthful sophistication. They serve up pricey but nicely executed Swedish and international dishes in their winter garden, bright dining room, and white-tile-and-wine-glass-chandeliered bar (Mon-Fri 7:30-24:00, Sat-Sun from 11:00, Birger Jarlsgatan 4, tel. 08/5450-3560).

$$ Sushi Yama Express is a quick and tasty option for takeaway sushi, sashimi, and rolls (Mon-Fri 10:00-20:00, closed Sat-Sun, at Nybrogatan 18, tel. 08/202-031).

Stockholm Connections

BY BUS

Swebus is the largest operator of long-distance buses, which can be cheaper than trains (tel. 0771/21-8218, www.swebus.se); Nettbuss also has lots of routes (www.nettbuss.se). Some bus companies offer discounts with advance purchase.

From Stockholm by Bus to: Copenhagen (about 3/day with change in Malmö, 9.5 hours, longer for overnight trips), **Oslo** (3/day, 8 hours), **Kalmar** (3/day, fewer on weekends, 6 hours).

BY TRAIN

The easiest and cheapest way to book train tickets is online at www.sj.se. Simply select your journey, pay with a credit card, and print out your ticket. You can also buy or print tickets at the station, using a self-service kiosk (bring your purchase confirmation code). If you need help, tickets are sold at a desk at bigger stations, but this can come with long lines and a surcharge. For timetables and prices, check online, call 0771/757-575, or use self-service ticket kiosks.

As with airline tickets and hotel rooms, Swedish train ticket prices vary with demand. The cheapest are advance-purchase, nonchangeable, and nonrefundable.

For rail-pass holders, seat reservations are required on express (such as the "SJ high-speed" class) and overnight trains, and they're recommended on some longer routes (to Oslo, for example). If you have a rail pass, make your seat reservation at a ticket window in a train station, by phone (at the number above), or online.

From Stockholm by Train to: Uppsala (4/hour, 40 minutes; also possible on slower suburban *pendeltåg*—2/hour, 55 minutes, covered by local transit pass plus small supplement), **Växjö** (almost hourly, 3.5 hours, change in Alvesta, reservations required), **Kalmar** (almost hourly, 4.5-5 hours, transfer in Alvesta, reservations required), **Copenhagen** (almost hourly, 5-6 hours on high-speed train, some with a transfer at Lund or Hässleholm, reservations required; overnight train requires a change in Malmö or Lund; all trains stop at Copenhagen airport before terminating at the central train station).

By Train to Oslo: The speedy X2000 train zips from downtown Copenhagen to downtown Oslo in about 5.5 hours, runs several times daily, and requires reservations (160 NOK in first class, 65 NOK in second class; first class often comes with a hot meal, fruit bowl, and unlimited coffee). Note that through 2020, construction on this line will likely interrupt service, in which case you'll take the slower SJ InterCity train (recommended 35-NOK reservation in either class). There may also be (slower) connections possible with a change in Göteborg.

BY OVERNIGHT BOAT

Ferry boat companies run shuttle buses from the train station to coincide with each departure; check for details when you buy your ticket. When comparing prices between boats and planes, remember that the boat fare includes a night's lodging.

From Stockholm to: Helsinki and **Tallinn** (daily/nightly boats, 16 hours, **Turku** (daily/nightly boats, 11-12 hours). The St. Peter Line connects Stockholm to **St. Petersburg,** but the trip takes two nights—you'll sail the first night to Tallinn, then a second night to St. Petersburg; returning, you'll sail the first night to Helsinki, and the second night to Stockholm (www.stpeterline. com). Note: To visit Russia, American and Canadian citizens need a visa (arrange weeks in advance).

BY CRUISE SHIP

For many more details on Stockholm's ports, and other cruise destinations, pick up my *Rick Steves Scandinavian & Northern European Cruise Ports* guidebook.

Stockholm has two cruise ports: the more central **Stadsgården,** used mainly by ships that are just passing through, is in Södermalm; **Frihamnen,** used primarily by ships beginning or ending a cruise in Stockholm, is three miles northeast of the city center.

Getting Downtown: Most cruise lines offer a convenient **shuttle bus** (about 120 SEK round-trip) that drops you in downtown Stockholm (likely near the Opera House). From there it's an easy walk or public bus/tram ride to the sights. **Taxis** from each port are also available (depending on your destination, figure 165-220 SEK from Stadsgården and 200-300 SEK from Frihamnen). Other options, including a hop-on, hop-off bus or boat from Stadsgården or the public bus from Frihamnen, are explained later.

Port Details: TI kiosks (with bus tickets, city guides, and maps) open at both ports when ships arrive.

Stadsgården is a long embankment, with cruises arriving at areas that flank the busy Viking Line Terminal (used by boats to Helsinki). The nearest transportation hub (with bus and T-bana stops) is Slussen, which sits beneath the bridge connecting the Old Town/Gamla Stan and the Södermalm neighborhood. Berth 160 is an easy 15-minute **walk** to Slussen; berth 167 is farther out but still walkable (about 30 minutes to Slussen).

From Stadsgården, a good option is the handy **hop-on, hop-off harbor boat** tour, which stops near both berths and connects to worthwhile downtown areas for a reasonable price (tickets often discounted from cruise port). **Taxis** and **hop-on, hop-off tour**

buses are also available (for details on all these options, see "Tours in Stockholm," earlier).

Frihamnen is a sprawling port zone used by cruise liners as well as overnight boats to St. Petersburg (boats to Tallinn, Helsinki, and Riga go from nearby Värtahamnen). Cruises typically use one of three berths—634, 638, or 650. Berth 638 is the main dock and has a dedicated terminal building (with a TI desk and gift shops). Along the main harborfront road you'll find a TI kiosk; hop-on, hop-off bus tours (for details see "Tours in Stockholm," earlier); and a public **bus** stop—a good option. Bus #76 zips you to several major sights, including Djurgårdsbron, Nybroplan, Kungsträdgården, Räntmästartrappan, and Slussen (4-7/hour Mon-Fri, 3-4/hour Sat-Sun). **Bus #1** cuts across the top of Östermalm and Norrmalm to the train station (every 5-8 minutes daily). You can't buy bus tickets on board—get one at the TI inside the terminal, at the booth near the bus stop, from the ticket machine at the bus stop, or use the handy SL ticketing app (called "SL-Stockholm"; see "Getting Around Stockholm," earlier).

BY PLANE

For information on arriving at Stockholm's airports, see "Arrival in Stockholm," earlier in this chapter.

NEAR STOCKHOLM

Drottningholm Palace • Sigtuna • Uppsala

At Stockholm's doorstep is a variety of fine side-trip options—all within an hour of the capital. Drottningholm Palace, on the city's outskirts, was the summer residence—and most opulent castle—of the Swedish royal family, and has a uniquely well-preserved Baroque theater, to boot. The adorable town of Sigtuna is a cutesy, cobbled escape from the big city, studded with history and rune stones. Uppsala is Sweden's answer to Oxford, offering stately university facilities and museums, the home and garden of scientist Carl Linnaeus, as well as a grand cathedral and the enigmatic burial mounds of Gamla Uppsala on the outskirts of town. Note that another side-trip option is to visit a few of the islands in Stockholm's archipelago (described in the next chapter).

Drottningholm Palace

The queen's 17th-century summer castle and current royal residence has been called "Sweden's Versailles." While that's a bit of a stretch, taken as a whole the Drottningholm Palace complex (Drottningholms Slott) is worth ▲▲. It's enjoyable to explore the place where the Swedish royals bunk and to stroll their expansive gardens. Even more worthwhile is touring the Baroque-era theater on the grounds (itself rated ▲▲), which preserves 18th-century stage sets and rare special-effects machinery. If you've seen plenty of palaces, skip the interior but enjoy the grounds and theater tour. You can likely squeeze everything in with half a day here, or linger for an entire day.

GETTING THERE

Drottingholm is an easy boat or subway-plus-bus ride from downtown Stockholm. Consider approaching by water (as the royals traditionally did) and then re-

turning by bus and subway (as a commoner). If your heart is set on touring the palace interior, check the website before you go: It can close unexpectedly for various events.

Boats depart regularly from the Klara Malarstrand pier just across from City Hall for the relaxing hour-long trip (160 SEK one-way, 210 SEK round-trip, on the hour daily, likely additional departures at :30 past the hour on weekends or any day in July-Aug, fewer departures Sept-April, tel. 08/1200-4000, www.stromma.se). The pier is a five-minute walk from the central train station (on Vasagatan, walk toward the water, staying to the right and crossing a plaza under the freeway to reach the pier). It's worth reserving a spot in advance on weekends, or if your day plan requires a particular departure.

It's faster (30-45 minutes total) to take **public transit:** Ride the T-bana about 20 minutes to Brommaplan, where you can catch any #300-series bus for the five-minute ride to Drottningholm (as you leave the Brommaplan station, check monitors to see which bus is leaving next—usually from platform A, E, or F).

BACKGROUND

"Drottningholm" means "Queen's Island." When the original castle mysteriously burned down in 1661 immediately after a visit

from Queen Hedvig Eleonora, she (quite conveniently) had already commissioned plans for a bigger, better palace.

Built over 40 years—with various rooms redecorated by centuries of later monarchs—Drottningholm has the air of overcompensating for an inferiority complex. While rarely absolute rulers, Sweden's royals long struggled with stubborn parliaments. Perhaps this made the propaganda value of the palace decor even more important. Touring the palace, you'll see art that makes the point that Sweden's royalty is divine and belongs with the gods. Portraits and prominently displayed gifts from fellow monarchs attempt to legitimize the royal family by connecting the Swedish blue bloods with Roman emperors, medieval kings, and Europe's great royal

families. The portraits you'll see of France's Louis XVI and Russia's Catherine the Great are reminders that Sweden's royalty was related to or tightly networked with the European dynasties.

Of course, today's monarchs are figureheads ruled by a constitution. The royal family makes a point to be as accessible and as "normal" as royalty can be. King Carl XVI Gustaf (b. 1946)—whose main job is handing out Nobel Prizes once a year—is a car nut who talks openly about his dyslexia. He was the first Swedish king not to be crowned "by the grace of God." At his 1976 wedding to the popular Queen Silvia, ABBA serenaded his bride with "Dancing Queen." Their daughter Crown Princess Victoria is heir to the throne (she studied political science at Yale, interned with Sweden's European Union delegation, and married her personal trainer, Daniel Westling, in 2010). The king and queen still live in one wing of Drottningholm, while other members of the royal family attempt to live more "normal" lives elsewhere.

SIGHTS AT DROTTNINGHOLM
Drottningholm Palace

While not the finest palace interior in Europe (or even in Scandinavia), Drottningholm offers a chance to stroll through a place where a monarch still lives. You'll see two floors of lavish rooms, where Sweden's royalty did their best to live in the style of Europe's divine monarchs.

Cost and Hours: 130 SEK, combo-ticket with Chinese Pavilion-190 SEK; May-Sept daily 10:00-16:30, April until 15:30, rest of year open weekends only—see website for hours, closed last two weeks of Dec.

Information: Tel. 08/402-6280, www.kungahuset.se.

Tours: You can explore the palace on your own, but with sparse posted explanations and no audioguide, it's worth the 30 SEK extra for the 30-minute English guided tour. Tours are offered daily, usually at 10:00, 12:00, 14:00, and 16:00 (fewer tours Oct-May). Alternatively, you could buy the inexpensive palace guidebook.

Services: The gift shop/café at the entrance to the grounds (near the boat dock and bus stop) acts as a visitors center; Drottningholm's only WCs are in the adjacent building. A handy Pressbyrån convenience store is also nearby (snacks, drinks, and transit tickets), and taxis are usually standing by.

Visiting Drottningholm Palace: Ascend the grand staircase (decorated with faux marble and relief-illusion paintings) and buy your ticket on the first floor. Entering the staterooms on the **first floor,** admire the craftsmanship of the walls, with gold leaf shimmering on expertly tooled leather. Then pass through the Green Cabinet and hook right into Hedvig Eleonora's State Bed Chambers. The richly colored Baroque decor here, with gold embellishments, is representative of what the entire interior once looked like. Hedvig Eleonora was a "dowager queen," meaning that she was the widow of a king—her husband, King Karl X, died young at age 24—after they had been married just six years. Looking around the room, you'll see symbolism of this tragic separation. For example, in the ceiling painting, Hedvig Eleonora rides a cloud, with hands joined below her—suggesting that she will be reunited with her beloved in heaven.

This room was also the residence of a later monarch, Gustav III. That's why it looks like (and was) more of a theater than a place for sleeping. In the style of the French monarchs, this is where the ceremonial tucking-in and dressing of the king would take place.

Backtrack into the golden room, then continue down the other hallway. You'll pass through a room of royal portraits with very consistent characteristics: pale skin with red cheeks; a high forehead with gray hair (suggesting wisdom); and big eyes (windows to the soul). At the end of the hall is a grand library, which once held some 7,000 books. The small adjoining room is filled by a large model of a temple in Pompeii; Gustav III—who ordered this built—was fascinated by archaeology, and still today, there's a museum of antiquities named for him at the Royal Palace in Stockholm.

On the **second floor,** as you enter the first room, notice the faux doors, painted on the walls to create symmetry, and the hidden doors for servants (who would scurry—unseen and unheard—through the walls to attend to the royal family). In the Blue Drawing Room is a bust of the then-king's cousin, Catherine the Great. This Russian monarch gave him—in the next room, the Chinese Drawing Room—the (made-in-Russia) faux "Chinese" stove. This dates from a time when exotic imports from China (tea, silk, ivory, Kung Pao chicken) were exciting and new. (Around the same time, in the mid-18th century, the royals built the Chinese Pavilion on Drottningholm's grounds.) The Gobelins tapestries in this room were also a gift, from France's King Louis XVI. In the next room, the darker Oskar Room, are more tapestries—these a gift from England's King Charles I. (Sensing a trend?) You'll pass through Karl XI's Gallery (overlooking the grand staircase)—which is still used for royal functions—and into the largest room on this floor, the Hall of State. The site of royal weddings and receptions, this room boasts life-size paintings of very important Swedes in golden frames and a bombastically painted ceiling.

Drottningholm Palace Park

Like so many European "summer palaces," the Drottningholm grounds are graced with sprawling gardens that are a pretty place to stroll on a fine day. Directly behind the palace is the strictly geometrical Baroque Garden, with angular hedges, tidy rows of trees, fountains, and outdoor "rooms" at the far end. It adjoins the more naturalistic English Garden, which Gustav III was determined to have after seeing one of the landscape gardens belonging to his cousin Catherine the Great. (It was  Gustav, too, who speckled the grounds with marble statues.) At the far end of the grounds is the Chinese Pavilion, containing a fine Rococo interior with chinoiserie.

Drottningholm Court Theater

This 18th-century theater (Drottningholms Slottsteater) has miraculously survived the ages—complete with its instruments, original stage sets, and hand-operated sound-effects machines for wind, thunder, and clouds. The required guided tour is short (30 minutes), entertaining, and informative—I found it more enjoyable than the palace tour.

Cost and Hours: 100 SEK for 30-minute guided tour—buy tickets in the theater shop next door, English tours about hourly May-Aug 11:00-16:30, Sept 12:00-15:30—these are first and last tour times, limited tours possible on weekends in April and Oct-Dec, no tours Jan-March.

Information: Tel. 08/759-0406, www.dtm.se.

Performances: Check their schedule for the rare opportunity to see perfectly authentic operas (about 25 performances each summer). Tickets for this popular time-travel musical and theatrical experience cost 300-1,000 SEK and go on sale each March; purchase online (www.ticktmaster.se), at the theater shop, or by phone (from the US, call +46-77-170-7070; see theater website for details).

Background: A Swedish king built the theater in the mid-1700s to pacify his Prussian wife, who was appalled by the provincialism of Sweden's performing arts. This is one of two such historic theaters remaining in Europe (the other is in the Czech town of Český Krumlov). Their son, King Gustav III, loved the theater (some say more than he loved ruling Sweden): Besides ordering Stockholm's Royal Opera to be built, he also wrote, directed, and acted in several theatrical presentations (including the first-ever production in Swedish instead of French, the usual court language). He even died in a theater, assassinated at a masquerade ball in the very opera house he had built. When he died, so too did this flourishing of culture: The theater became a warehouse for storing royal bric-a-brac. The stage stayed dark until the mid-1940s, when opera and plays were once again performed here.

Visiting the Theater: On the tour, you'll see the bedrooms where famous actors and conductors would sleep while performing here, then enter the theater itself, lit only with (now simulated) candles. You'll see the extremely deep stage (with scenery peeking in from the edges), the royal boxes where the king and queen entered, and doors and curtains that were painted onto walls to achieve perfect symmetry.

It's fascinating to think that the system of pulleys, trap doors, and actors floating in from the sky isn't so different from the techniques employed on stages today. Because the mechanisms are fragile, they aren't demonstrated on the tour, but you can watch a video demonstration in the theater shop next door.

NEAR STOCKHOLM

Sigtuna

Sigtuna, the oldest town in Sweden (established in the 970s), is the country's cutest town as well. Worth ▲, it sits sugary sweet on Lake Mälaren, about 30 miles inland from Stockholm (reachable by train/bus or sightseeing boat). A visit here affords a relaxed look at an open-air folk museum of a town, with ruined churches, ancient rune stones, and a lane of 18th-century buildings—all with English info posts. It also offers plenty of shopping and eating options in a parklike lakeside setting. If you're looking for stereotypical Sweden and a break from the big city, Sigtuna is a fun side-trip.

Getting There: By **public transport** from Stockholm, it's a one-hour trip. Take the *pendeltåg* suburban train from Stockholm to Märsta and then change to bus #570 or #575. You can buy all four train and bus tickets needed for a round-trip journey in Stockholm—just scan the ticket for each leg at the sensor before boarding each train or bus (but be alert that you can accidentally validate all at once if you stack them and scan the one on top).

Guided two-hour **sightseeing cruises** run to Sigtuna in summer (375 SEK round-trip, Wed-Sun morning departures from Stockholm's Stadshusbron dock, www.stromma.se). If traveling by **car** to Uppsala or Oslo, Sigtuna is a short detour.

Tourist Information: The helpful TI is on the main street and eager to equip you with a town map (daily 10:00-17:00, Storagatan 33, tel. 08/5948-0650, http://destinationsigtuna.se/en/).

Sights in Sigtuna

Main Street: Storagatan

Sigtuna's main street provides the town's spine. Along it, besides the TI, you'll find the Town Hall from 1744, with a nicely preserved interior (free, June-Aug daily 12:00-16:00), and the Sigtuna History Museum, with archaeological finds from the Viking culture here (may be closed for renovation). As you stroll the street, read the historical signs posted along the way and poke into shops and cafés. The most charming place for lunch, a snack, or a drink is Tant Brun ("Auntie Brown's") Café, tucked away just around the corner from the TI in a super-characteristic 17th-century home with a cozy garden.

Churches

Before the Reformation came along, Sigtuna was an important political and religious center, and the site of the country's archbishopric. Along with powerful monastic communities, the town had seven churches. When the Reformation hit, that was the end of the monasteries, and there was a need for only one church—the Gothic Mariakyrkan. It survived, and the rest fell into ruins. Mariakyrkan, or Mary's Church, built by the Dominicans in the 13th century, is decorated with pre-Reformation murals and is worth a look (free, daily 9:00-17:00).

The stony remains of St. Olaf's Church stand in the Mary's Church cemetery. This 12th-century ruin is evocative, with stout vaults and towering walls that served the community as a place of last refuge when under attack.

Rune Stones

Sigtuna is dotted with a dozen rune stones. Literally "word stones," these memorial stones are carved with messages in an Iron Age runic language. Sigtuna has more of these than any other Swedish town. Those here generally have a cross, indicating that they are from the Christian era (11th century). Each is described in English. I like Anund's stone, which says, "Anund had this stone erected in memory of himself in his lifetime." His rune carver showed a glimpse of personality and that perhaps Anund had no friends. (It worked. Now he's in an American guidebook, and 10 centuries later, he's still remembered.)

Uppsala

Uppsala, Sweden's fourth-largest city, is a rather small town with a big history. A few blocks in front of its train station, an inviting commercial center bustles around the main square and along a scenic riverfront. Towering across the river are its historic cathedral and a venerable university. For visitors, the university features a rare 17th-century anatomical theater, an exhibit of its prestigious academic accomplishments, and a library with literary treasures on display. Uppsala is home to the father of modern botany, Carl Linnaeus, whose garden and house—now a museum—make for a fascinating visit. And, just outside town stands Gamla Uppsala, the site of a series of majestic burial mounds where Sweden buried its royalty back in the 6th century. While Gamla Uppsala is a short bus ride away, everything else is within delightful walking distance. If you're not traveling anywhere else in Sweden other than Stockholm, Uppsala (less than an hour away) makes a pleasant day

NEAR STOCKHOLM

trip. While buzzing during the school year, this university town is sleepy during summer vacations.

GETTING THERE

Take the train from Stockholm's central station (5/hour, 40 minutes, 85 SEK; also possible on slower suburban *pendeltåg*—2/hour, 55 minutes, covered by local transit pass plus small supplement). Since the Uppsala station has lockers and is in the same direction from Stockholm as the airport, you could combine a quick visit here with an early arrival or late departure.

Orientation to Uppsala

TOURIST INFORMATION

The helpful TI, across the street from the train station, has the informative *What's On Uppsala* magazine, which includes the best map of the center and a list of sights (Mon-Fri 10:00-17:00, Sat until 15:00, Sun July-Aug only 11:00-15:00, Kungsgatan 59, tel. 018/727-4800, www.destinationuppsala.se).

ARRIVAL IN UPPSALA

From the train station (pay lockers), cross the busy street and find the TI on the right (pick up the *What's On* magazine). Walk two blocks to Kungsängsgatan, turn right, and walk to the main square,

Stora Torget. The spires of the cathedral mark two of the top three sights (the cathedral itself and the adjacent university buildings). The Linnaeus Garden and Museum is a few blocks up the river, and the bus to Gamla Uppsala is a couple of blocks away.

Sights in Uppsala

▲▲Uppsala Cathedral
(Uppsala Domkyrkan)

One of Scandinavia's largest, most historic cathedrals feels as vital as it does impressive. While the building was completed in 1435, the spires and interior decorations are from the late 19th century. The cathedral—with a fine Gothic interior, the relics of St. Erik, memories of countless Swedish coronations, and the tomb of King Gustav Vasa—is well worth a visit.

Cost and Hours: Free, daily 8:00-18:00; free guided English tours go 1-2 times/day in season (mid-June-mid-Aug Mon-Sat at 11:00 and 14:00, Sun at 15:00), or pick up brochure in gift shop; tel. 018/187-177, www.uppsaladomkyrka.se.

Visiting the Cathedral: Grab a seat in a pew and take in the graceful Gothic lines of the longest nave in Scandinavia (130 yards). The gorgeously carved, gold-slathered Baroque pulpit is a reminder of the Protestant (post-Reformation) focus on preaching the word of God in the people's language. Look high above in the choir area to enjoy fine murals, restored in the 1970s. For ages, pilgrims have come here to see the relics of St. Erik. All around you are important side chapels, tombs, and memorials (each with an English description).

Near the entrance is the tomb and memorial to scientist Carl Linnaeus, the father of modern botany, who spent his career at the university here (for more on him, see the Linnaeus Garden and Museum listing, later).

In the chapel at the far east end of the church is the tomb of King Gustav Vasa and his family. This chapel was originally dedicated to the Virgin Mary. But Gustav Vasa brought the Reformation to Sweden in 1527 and usurped this prized space for his own tomb. In good Swedish style, the decision was affirmed by a vote in parliament, and bam—the country was Lutheran. (A few years later, England's King Henry VIII tried a similar religious revolution—and had a much tougher time.) Notice that in the tomb sculpture, Gustav is shown flanked by two wives—his first wife died after suffering a fall; his second wife bore him 10 children. High above are murals of Gustav's illustrious life.

Speaking of Mary, notice the modern statue of a common-rather-than-regal Protestant Mary outside the chapel looking in. This eerily lifelike statue from 2005, called *Mary (The Return),* captures Jesus' mother wearing a scarf and timeless garb. In keeping with the Protestant spirit here, this new version of Mary is shown not as an exalted queen, but as an everywoman, saddened by the loss of her child and seeking solace—or answers—in the church.

Cathedral Treasury: By the gift shop, you can pay to ride the elevator up to the treasury collection. Here (with the help of a loaner flashlight and English translations), you'll find medieval textiles (tapestries and vestments), swords and crowns found in Gustav's grave, and the Nobel Peace Prize won by Nathan Söderblom, an early-20th-century archbishop here (40 SEK, daily 10:00-17:00, until 16:00 off-season). In this same narthex area, notice the debit-card machine for offerings.

Eating: The **$$ Cathedral Café** (a few steps to the right as you exit the cathedral) is charming, reasonable, and handy—and your money supports the city's mission of helping the local homeless population (lunch specials, Mon-Fri 10:00-16:30, Sat-Sun 11:00-16:00). Or, survey the many eateries on or near the main square or along the river below the cathedral.

UNIVERSITY AND NEARBY

Scandinavia's first university was founded in Uppsala in 1477. Two famous grads are Carl Linnaeus (the famous botanist) and Anders Celsius (the scientist who developed the temperature scale that bears his name). The campus is scattered around the cathedral part of town, and two university buildings are particularly interesting and welcoming to visitors: the Gustavianum and the library.

▲▲Gustavianum

Facing the cathedral is the university's oldest surviving building, with a bulbous dome that doubles as a sundial (notice the gold numbers). Today it houses a well-presented museum that features an anatomical theater, a cabinet filled with miniature curiosities, and Celsius' thermometer. The collection is curiously engaging for the glimpse it gives into the mindset of 17th-century Europe.

Cost and Hours: 50 SEK, Tue-Sun 10:00-16:00, Sept-May from 11:00, closed Mon year-round, Akademigatan 3, tel. 018/471-7571, www.gustavianum.uu.se.

Visiting the Gustavianum: Ride the elevator (near the gift shop/ticket desk) up to the fourth floor. Then, see the exhibits as you walk back down.

Up top is a collection of **Viking artifacts** discovered at Valsgärde, a prehistoric site near Uppsala used for burials for more than 700 years. Archaeologists have uncovered 15 boat graves here (dating from A.D. 600-1050—roughly one per generation), providing insight on the Viking Age. The recovered artifacts on display here show fine Viking workmanship and a society more refined than many might expect.

Next you'll find the **anatomical theater** (accessible from the fourth and third floors). This theater's only show was human dissection. In the mid-1600s, as the enlightened ideas of the Renaissance swept far into the north of Europe, scholars began to consider dissection of the human body the ultimate scientific education. Corpses of hanged criminals were carefully sliced and diced here, under a dome in an almost temple-like atmosphere, demonstrating the lofty heights to which science had risen in society. Imagine 200 students standing tall all around and leaning in to peer intently at the teacher's scalpel. Notice the plaster death masks of the dissected in a case at the entry.

On the second floor is a fascinating exhibit on the **history of the university.** The Physics Chamber features a collection of instruments from the 18th and 19th centuries that were used by university teachers. The Augsburg Art Cabinet takes center stage here with a dizzying array of nearly 1,000 minuscule works of art and other tidbits held in an ornately decorated oak cabinet. Built in the 1620s for a bigwig who wanted to impress his friends, the cabinet once held the items now shown in the display cases surrounding it. Find the interactive video screen, where you can control a virtual tour of the collection. Just beyond the cabinet is a thermometer that once belonged to Celsius (in his handwriting, notice how 0 and 100 were originally flip-flopped, with water boiling at 0 degrees Celsius rather than 100).

On the first floor is the university's **classical antiquities collection** from the Mediterranean. These ancient Greek and Roman artifacts and Egyptian sarcophagi were used to bring classical culture and art to students unable to travel abroad.

▲University Library (Universitetsbiblioteket)

Uppsala University's library, housed in a 19th-century building called the Carolina Rediviva, is a block uphill from the cathedral and Gustavianum. Off the entry hall (to the right) is a small but exquisite exhibit of treasured old books. Well-displayed and well-described in English, the carefully selected collection is surprisingly captivating.

Cost and Hours: Free, daily 9:00-18:00, Dag Hammarskjölds väg 1, tel. 018/471-1000, www.ub.uu.se.

Visiting the Library: With precious items like Mozart scores in the composer's own hand, margin notes by Copernicus in a 13th-century astronomy book, and a map of Mexico City dating from 1555, the display cases here feel like the Treasures room at the British Library.

The most valuable item is the **Silver Bible,** a translation from Greek of the four Gospels into the now-extinct Gothic language. Written in Ravenna in the 6th century, Sweden's single most precious book is so named for its silver-ink writing on purple-colored calfskin vellum. Booty from a 1648 Swedish victory in Prague, it ended up at Uppsala University in 1669.

Another rarity is the **Carta Marina,** the first more-or-less accurate map of Scandinavia, printed in Venice in 1539 from nine woodblocks. Compare this 16th-century understanding of the region with your own travels.

▲Linnaeus Garden and Museum (Linnéträdgården)

Carl Linnaeus, famous for creating the formal system for naming different species of plants and animals, spent his career in Uppsala as a professor. This home, office, greenhouse, and garden is the ultimate Linnaeus sight, providing a vivid look at this amazing scientist and his work.

Cost and Hours: 80 SEK for museum and garden; museum open daily 11:00-17:00 except closed Mon in May, Mon-Thu in Sept, and Oct-April; garden open until 20:00; daily 45-minute English tour at 14:30; after 17:00, when the museum closes, the garden becomes a free public space—enter on Svartbäcksgatan at #27; tel. 018/471-2874, www.linnaeus.uu.se.

Visiting the Garden and Museum: While Linnaeus (whose noble name was Carl von Linné) was professor of medicine and botany at the University of Uppsala, he lived and studied here. From 1743 until 1778, he ran this botanical garden and lived on site to study the plant action—day and night, year-round—of about 3,000 different species. When he moved in, the university's department of medicine and botany moved in as well.

It was in this garden (the first in Sweden, originally set up in 1655) that Linnaeus developed a way to classify the plant kingdom. Wandering the garden where the most famous of all botanists did his work, you can pop into the orangery, built so temperate plants could survive the Nordic winters.

The museum, in Linnaeus' home (which he shared with his wife and seven children), is filled with the family's personal possessions and his professional gear. You'll see his insect cabinet, herbs cabinet, desk, botany tools, and notes. An included audioguide helps bring the exhibit to life.

More Sights near the University

Uppsala has a range of lesser sights, all within walking distance of the cathedral. The **Uppland Museum** (Upplandsmuseet), a regional history museum with prehistoric bits and folk-art scraps, is on the river by the waterfall, near the TI (free, Tue-Sun 12:00-17:00, closed Mon). Uphill from the university library is the 16th-century **Uppsala Castle,** which houses an art museum and runs slice-of-castle-life tours (inquire at TI, tel. 018/727-2485).

ON THE OUTSKIRTS
▲Gamla Uppsala

This pleasant, scenic site on the outskirts of town gives historians goose bumps. Gamla Uppsala—literally, "Old Uppsala"—includes

nine large royal burial mounds circled by a walking path. Fifteen hundred years ago, when the Baltic Sea was higher and it was easy to sail all the way to Uppsala, the pagan Swedish kings had their capital here. Old Uppsala is where the Swedish kingdoms came together and a nation coalesced.

Cost and Hours: The **mounds** are free and always open. The **museum** is 80 SEK and open daily 11:00-17:00 (shorter hours Sept-March—generally 12:00-16:00 and closed Tue, Wed, and Fri). In summer your museum admission includes a 40-minute guided English tour of the mounds (July-Aug daily at 12:30 and 15:30, tel. 018/239-312, www.raa.se/gamlauppsala). The **church** is free and open daily 9:00-18:00, Sept-March until 16:00 (tiny church museum across the lane is free and open Sat-Sun only 12:00-15:00).

Getting There: A direct city bus stops right at the site. From the Uppsala train station, go to the bus stop on the town square (Stora Torget, 2 blocks away) and take bus #2, marked *Gamla Uppsala,* to the last stop—Kungshögarna (35 SEK if bought on board—credit cards only, otherwise buy ticket at Pressbyrån kiosk on the square; 2-4/hour, 15-minute trip). All the Gamla Uppsala sights are within 200 yards of each other, making it an easy visit.

Eating: Gamla Uppsala is great for picnics, or you can drop by the rustic and half-timbered **$** Odinsborg café, which serves sandwiches, mead, and daily specials (daily 10:00-18:00, tel. 018/323-525).

Visiting Gamla Uppsala: The highlight of a visit is to climb the evocative mounds, which you're welcome to wander. Also at the site is a small but interesting museum and a 12th-century church.

The Mounds: The focus of ritual and religious activities from the 6th through 13th centuries, the mounds are made meaningful with the help of English info boards posted around.

Imagine the scene over a thousand years ago, when the democratic tradition of this country helped bring the many small Swedish kingdoms together into one nation. A *ting* was a political assembly where people dealt with the issues of the day. Communities would gather here at the rock that marked their place, and then the leader, standing atop the flat mound (nearest today's café), would address the crowd as if in a natural amphitheater. It was here that Sweden became Christianized a thousand years ago. In 1989 Pope John Paul II gave a Mass right here to celebrate the triumph of Christianity over paganism in Sweden. (These days, this is a pretty secular society and relatively few Swedes go to church.)

Museum: Gamla Uppsala's museum gives a good overview of early Swedish history and displays items found in the mounds. While humble, it is instructive, with plenty of excavated artifacts.

Church: Likely standing upon a pagan holy site, the church dates from the 12th century and was the residence of the first Swedish archbishop. An 11th-century rune stone is embedded in the external wall. In the entryway, an iron-clad oak trunk with seven locks on it served as the church treasury back in the 12th century. In the nave, a few Catholic frescoes, whitewashed over in the 16th century with the Reformation, have been restored.

STOCKHOLM'S ARCHIPELAGO

Vaxholm • Grinda • Svartsö • Sandhamm

Some of Europe's most scenic islands stretch 80 miles out into the Baltic Sea from Stockholm. If you're cruising to (or from) Finland, you'll get a good look at this island beauty. If you have more time and want to immerse yourself in all that simple Swedish nature, consider spending a day or two island-hopping.

The Swedish word for "island" is simply *ö*, but the local name for this area is Skärgården—literally, "garden of skerries," which are unforested rocks sticking up from the sea. That stone is granite, carved out and deposited by glaciers. The archipelago closer to Stockholm is rockier, with bigger islands and more trees. Farther out (such as at Sandhamn), the glaciers lingered longer, slowly grinding the granite into sand and creating smaller islands.

Locals claim there are more than 30,000 of these islands, and as land here is rising slowly, more pop out every year. Some 150 are inhabited year-round, and about 100 have ferry service. There's an unwritten law of public access in the archipelago: Technically you're allowed to pitch your tent anywhere for up to two nights, provided the owner of the property can't see you from his or her house. It's polite to ask first and essential to act responsibly.

With thousands of islands to choose from, every Swede seems to have a favorite. This chapter covers four very different island destinations that offer an overview of the archipelago. Vaxholm, the gateway to the archipelago, comes with an imposing fortress, a charming fishermen's harbor, and the easiest connections to Stockholm. Rustic Grinda feels like—and used to be—a Swedish summer camp. Sparsely populated Svartsö is another fine back-to-nature experience. And swanky Sandhamn thrills the sailboat set, with a lively yacht harbor, a scenic setting at the far edge of the archipelago, and (true to its name) sandy beaches.

The flat-out best way to experience the magic of the archipelago is simply stretching out comfortably on the rooftop deck of your ferry. The journey truly is the destination. Enjoy the charm of lovingly painted cottages as you glide by, sitting in the sun on delicate pairs of lounge chairs that are positioned to catch just the right view, with the steady rhythm of the ferries lacing this world together, and people savoring quality time with each other and nature.

PLANNING YOUR TIME

On a Tour: For the best quick look, consider one of the many half- or full-day package boat trips from downtown Stockholm to the archipelago. **Strömma** runs several options, including the three-hour Archipelago Tour (2-4/day, 280 SEK), or the all-day Thousand Island Cruise (departs daily in summer at 9:30, 1,235 SEK, includes lunch and dinner; tel. 08/1200-4000, www.stromma.se).

On Your Own: For more flexibility, freedom, and a better dose of the local vacation scene, do it on your own. Any one of the islands in this chapter is easily doable as a single-day side-trip from Stockholm. And, because all boats to and from Stockholm pass through Vaxholm, it's easy to tack on that town to any other one. For general information about the archipelago, see www.visitskargarden.se.

For a very busy all-day itinerary that takes in the two most enjoyable island destinations (Grinda and Sandhamn), consider this plan: 8:00—Set sail from Stockholm; 9:30—Arrive in Grinda for a quick walk around the island; 10:50—Catch the boat to Sandhamn; 11:45—Arrive in Sandhamn, have lunch, and enjoy the town; 17:00—Catch the boat to Stockholm (maybe have dinner on board); 19:05—Arrive back in Stockholm. Or you could craft a route tailored to your interests: For example, for a back-to-nature experience, try Stockholm-Grinda-Svartsö-Stockholm. For an urban mix of towns, consider Stockholm-Vaxholm-Sandhamn-Stockholm.

Overnighting on an island really lets you get away from it all and enjoy the island ambience. I've listed a few accommodations, but note that midrange options are few; most tend to be either pricey and top-end or very rustic (rented cottages with minimal plumbing).

Don't struggle too hard with the "which island?" decision. The

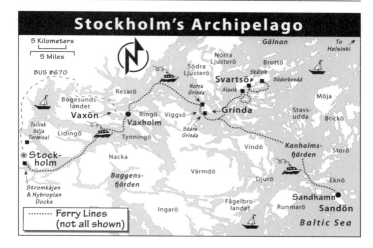

main thing is to get well beyond Vaxholm, where the scenery gets more striking. I'd sail an hour or two past Vaxholm, have a short stop on an island, then stop in Vaxholm on the way home. The real joy is the view from your ferry.

GETTING AROUND THE ARCHIPELAGO

A few archipelago destinations (including Vaxholm) are accessible overland, thanks to modern bridges. For other islands, you'll take

a boat. Two major companies run public ferries from downtown Stockholm to the archipelago: the bigger Waxholmsbolaget and the smaller Cinderella Båtarna.

Tickets: Regular tickets are sold on board. Simply walk on, and at your convenience, stop by the desk to buy your ticket before you disembark (or wait for them to come around and sell you one). Waxholmsbolaget offers a deal that's worthwhile if you're traveling with a small group or doing a lot of island-hopping. You can save 25 percent by buying a 1,000-SEK ticket credit for 750 SEK (sold only on land; use the splittable credit to buy tickets on the boat). If you're staying in the archipelago for a few days and want to island-hop, consider the Island Hopping Pass, a five-day, all-inclusive pass (445 SEK, plus a 20-SEK smartcard fee). Buy the card at the Waxholmsbolaget office.

Note that tickets and passes for the Waxholmsbolaget ferries are not valid on Cinderella Båtarna boats (and vice versa).

Schedules: Check both companies' schedules when planning your itinerary; you might have to mix and match to make your itinerary work. The most user-friendly option is to use the "Journey Planner" on www.waxholmsbolaget.se, which shows schedules for both companies. A single, confusing schedule booklet also mixes times for both lines. Ferry schedules are complex, and can be confusing even to locals, especially outside of peak season.

Note that the departures mentioned below are for summer (mid-June–mid-Aug); the number of boats declines off-season.

Waxholmsbolaget: Their ships depart from in front of Stockholm's Grand Hotel, at the stop called Stromkäjen (tel. 08/686-2465, www.waxholmsbolaget.se). Waxholmsbolaget boats run from Stockholm to, among other places, these islands: **Vaxholm** (at least hourly, 1.5 hours, 79 SEK), **Grinda** (nearly hourly, 2 hours, 95 SEK), **Svartsö** (3/day, 2.5 hours, 116 SEK), and **Sandhamn** (1/day, Sat-Sun only, 3.5 hours, 150 SEK). These destinations and their timetables are listed in the "Visitor" section of Waxholmsbolaget's website.

Cinderella Båtarna: These ships (operated by Strömma) focus their coverage on the most popular destinations. They're generally faster, make fewer stops, are more comfortable, and are a little pricier than their rivals (boats leave from near Stockholm's Nybroplan, along Strandvägen, tel. 08/1200-4045, www.stromma.se/stockholm/cinderellabatarna). Cinderella boats sail frequently (4/day Mon-Thu, 5/day Fri-Sun) from Stockholm to **Vaxholm** (50 minutes, 115 SEK) and **Grinda** (1.5 hours, 145 SEK). After Grinda, the line splits, going either to **Sandhamn** (from Stockholm: 1/day Mon-Thu, 2/day Fri-Sun, 2.5 hours, 165 SEK), or Finnhamn, with a stop en route at **Svartsö** (from Stockholm: 2/day, 2.5 hours, 165 SEK). These fares are for peak season (mid-June–mid-Aug); Cinderella's fares are slightly cheaper off-season.

On Board: When you board, tell the conductor which island you're going to. Boats don't land at all of the smaller islands unless passengers have requested a stop. Hang on to your ticket, as you'll have to show it to disembark. Some boats have luggage-storage areas (ask when you board).

You can usually access the outdoor deck; if you can't get to the front deck (where the boats load and unload), head to the back. Or nab a window seat inside. For the best seat, with less sun and nicer views, I'd go POSH: Port Out, Starboard Home (on the left side leaving Stockholm, on the right side coming back). As you sail, a monitor on board shows the position of your boat as it motors through the islands.

Food: You can usually buy food on board, ranging from simple fare at snack bars to elegant sea-view dinners at fancy restaurants. If your boat has a top-deck restaurant and you want to combine your cruise with dinner, make a reservation as soon as you board.

Once you have a table, it's yours for the whole trip, so you can simply claim your seat and enjoy the ride, circling back later to eat. You can also try calling ahead to reserve a table for a specific cruise (for Waxholmsbolaget, call 08/600-1000; for Cinderella, call 08/1200-4045).

HELPFUL HINTS

Tourist Information: Stockholm's city-run TI, called **Visit Stockholm,** has a free map of the archipelago, which gives a great overview and introduction to the area (downtown in the Kulturhuset, see hours and contact info in Stockholm chapter, under "Orientation to Stockholm").

Opening Times: Any opening hours I list in this chapter are reliable only for peak season (mid-June–mid-Aug). During the rest of the tourist year ("shoulder season"—late May, early June, late Aug, and Sept), hours are flexible and completely weather-dependent; more services tend to be open on weekends than weekdays. Outside the short summer season, many places close down entirely.

Money: Bring cash. The only ATMs are in Vaxholm; farther out, you'll wish you'd stocked up on cash in Stockholm, though most vendors do accept credit cards.

Signal for Stop: At the boat landings or jetties on small islands, you'll notice a small signal tower (called a semaphore) that's used to let a passing boat know you want to be picked up. Pull the cord to spin the white disc and make it visible to the ship. Be sure to put it back before boarding the boat. At night, you signal with light—locals just use their mobile phones.

Weather: The weather on the islands is often better than in Stockholm. For island forecasts, check Götland's (the big island far to the south) instead of Stockholm's. A good local website for weather forecasts (in English) is www.yr.no.

Local Drink: A popular drink here is *punsch,* a sweet fruit liqueur. Stately old buildings sometimes have *punsch–verandas,* little glassed-in upstairs porches where people traditionally would imbibe and chat.

ARCHIPELAGO

Vaxholm

The self-proclaimed "gateway to the archipelago," Vaxholm is more developed and less charming than the other islands. Connected by bridge to Stockholm, it's practically a suburb, and not the place to commune with Swedish nature. But it also has an illustrious history as the anchor of Stockholm's naval defense network, and it couldn't be easier to reach (constant buses and boats from Stockholm). While Vaxholm isn't the rustic archipelago you might be looking for, you're almost certain to pass through here at some point on your trip. If you have some extra time, hop off the boat for a visit.

Getting There: Boats constantly shuttle between Stockholm's waterfront and Vaxholm (see "Getting Around the Archipelago," earlier). **Bus #670** runs regularly from the Tekniska Högskolan T-bana stop in northern Stockholm to the center of Vaxholm (4/hour Mon-Fri, 3/hour Sat-Sun, 40 minutes, 43 SEK one-way, buy ticket in Pressbyrån convenience store across the street from station). Unless you're on a tight budget, I'd take the boat for the scenery.

Orientation to Vaxholm

Vaxholm, with about 5,000 people, is on the island of Vaxön, connected to the mainland (and Stockholm) by a series of bridges. Everything of interest is within a five-minute walk of the boat dock.

TOURIST INFORMATION

Vaxholm's good TI is well-stocked with brochures about Vaxholm itself, Stockholm, and the archipelago, and can help you with boat schedules (Mon-Fri 10:00-18:00, Sat-Sun until 16:00, shorter hours off-season; in the Town Hall building on Rådhustorget, tel. 08/5413-1480, www.vaxholm.se).

ARRIVAL IN VAXHOLM

Ferries stop at Vaxholm's south harbor (Söderhamnen). The **bus** from Stockholm arrives and departs at the bus stop called Söderhamnsplan, a few steps from the boats. To get your bearings, follow my Vaxholm Walk. Luggage lockers are in the Waxholmsbolaget building on the waterfront. The handy electronic departure board (*Nästa Avgang* means "next departure") near the ticket office shows when boats are leaving. For more help, confirm your plans with the person at the ticket office.

Vaxholm Walk

This 30-minute, self-guided, two-part loop will take you to the most characteristic corners of Vaxholm. Begin at the boat dock—you can even start reading as you approach.

Waterfront: Dominating Vaxholm's waterfront is the big Art Nouveau Waxholms Hotell, dating from the early 20th century.

Across the strait to the right is Vaxholm's stout fortress, a reminder of this town's strategic importance over the centuries.

With your back to the water, turn left and walk with the big hotel on your right-hand side. Notice the Waxholmsbolaget office building. Inside you can buy tickets, confirm boat schedules, or stow your bag in a locker. After the hamburger-and-hot-dog stand, you'll reach a roundabout. Just to your left is the stop for bus #670, connecting Vaxholm to Stockholm. Beyond that, a wooden walkway follows the seafront to the town's private boat harbor (Västerhamnen, or "west harbor"), where you can count sailboats and rent a bike.

But for now, continue straight up Vaxholm's appealing, shop-lined main street, Hamngatan. After one long block (notice the handy Co-op/Konsum grocery store across the street), turn right up Rådhusgatan (following signs to *Rådhustorget*) to reach the town's main square. The TI is inside the big, yellow Town Hall building on your left. Continue kitty-corner across the square (toward the granite slope) and head downhill on a street leading to the...

Fishermen's Quarter: This Norrhamnen ("north harbor") is ringed by former fishermen's homes. Walk out to the dock and survey the charming wooden cottages. In the mid-19th century, Stockholmers considered Vaxholm's herring, called *strömming,* top-quality. Caught fresh here, the herring could be rowed into the city in just eight hours and eaten immediately, while herring caught farther

out on the archipelago, which had to be preserved in salt, lost its flavor.

As you look out to sea, you'll see a pale green building protruding on the left. This is the charming Hembygdsgården homestead museum, with a pleasant indoor-outdoor café. It's worth heading to this little point (even if the museum is closed, as it often is): As you face the water, go left about one block, then turn right down the gravel lane called Trädgårdsgatan (also marked for *Hembygdsgården*).

Continuing down Trädgårdsgatan lane, you'll run right into the **Hembygdsgården homestead.** The big house features an endearing museum showing the simple, traditional fisherman's lifestyle (pop in if it's open; free but donation requested). Next door is a fine recommended café serving sweets and light meals with idyllic outdoor seating (both in front of and behind the museum—look around for your favorite perch, taking the wind direction into consideration). This is the best spot in town for coffee or lunch. From here, look across the inlet at the tiny beach (where we're heading next).

Backtrack to the fishermen's harbor, then continue straight uphill on Fiskaregatan road, and take the first left up the tiny gravel lane marked *Vallgatan.* This part of the walk takes you back in time, as you wander among old-fashioned wooden homes. At the end of the lane, head left. When you reach the water, go right along a path leading to a thriving little **sandy beach.** In good weather, this offers a fun chance to commune with Swedes at play. (In bad weather, it's hard to imagine anyone swimming or sunning here.)

When you're done relaxing, take the wooden stairs up to the top of the rock and **Battery Park** (Batteripark)—where giant artillery helped Vaxholm flex its defensive muscles in the late 19th century. As you crest the rock and enjoy the sea views, notice (on your right) the surviving semicircular tracks from those old artillery guns. With a range of 10 kilometers, the recoil from these powerful cannons could shatter glass in nearby houses. Before testing them, they'd play a bugle call to warn locals to stow away their valuables. More artifacts of these defenses are dug into the rock.

To head back to civilization, turn right before the embedded bunker (crossing more gun tracks and passing more fortifications on your left). As you leave the militarized zone, take a left at the fork, and the road will take you down to the embankment—just around the corner from where the boat docks, and our starting point. From along this stretch of embankment, you can catch a boat across the water to Vaxholm Fortress.

Sights in Vaxholm

Vaxholm Fortress and Museum
(Vaxholms Kastell/Vaxholms Fästnings Museum)

Vaxholm's only real attraction is the fortification just across the strait. While the town feels sleepy today, for centuries it was a crucial link in Sweden's nautical defense because it presided
over the most convenient passage between Stockholm and
the outer archipelago (and, beyond that, the Baltic Sea, Finland, and Russia). The name
"Vaxholm" means "Island of

the Signal Fire," emphasizing the burg's strategic importance. In 1548, King Gustav Vasa decided to pin his chances on this loca-
tion, ordering the construction of a fortress here and literally filling in other waterways, effectively making this the only way into or out of Stockholm...which it remained for 450 years. A village sprang up across the waterway to supply the fortress, and Vaxholm was born. The town's defenses successfully held off at least two major invasions (Christian IV of Denmark in 1612, and Peter the Great of Russia in 1719). Vaxholm's might gave Sweden's kings the peace of mind they needed to expand their capital to outlying islands—which means that the pint-size powerhouse of Vaxholm is largely to thank for Stockholm's island-hopping cityscape.

Cost and Hours: 80 SEK, July-Aug daily 11:00-17:00, June daily 12:00-16:00, May and Sept Sat-Sun from 12:00, closed off-season, tel. 08/1200-4870, www.vaxholmsfastning.se.

Getting There: A ferry shuttles visitors back and forth from Vaxholm (40 SEK round-trip, every 20 minutes when museum is open, catch the boat just around the corner and toward the fortress from where the big ferries put in). Once on the island, hike into the castle's inner courtyard and look to the left to find the museum entrance.

Visiting the Fortress: The current, "new" fortress dates from the mid-19th century, when an older castle was torn down and re-placed with this imposing granite behemoth. During the 30 years it took to complete the fortress, the tools of warfare changed. Both defensively and offensively, the new fortress was obsolete before it was even completed. The thick walls were no match for the in-vention of shells (rather than cannonballs), and the high hatches used for attacking tall sailing vessels were useless against new, low-lying, *Monitor*-style attack boats.

Today, the fortress welcomes guests to wander its tough little island and visit its museum. Presented chronologically on two floors (starting upstairs), the modern exhibit traces the military history of this fortress and of Sweden in general. It uses lots of models and mannequins, along with actual weaponry and artifacts, to tell the story right up to the 21st century. There's no English posted, but you can pick up good English translations as you enter. It's as interesting as a museum about Swedish military history can be.

Sleeping and Eating in Vaxholm

Since Vaxholm is so close to Stockholm, there's little reason to sleep here. But in a pinch, Waxholms is the only hotel in town.

Sleeping: $$$ Waxholms Hotell's stately Art Nouveau facade dominates the town's waterfront. Inside are 42 pleasant rooms with classy old-fashioned furnishings (loud music some nights in summer—ask what's on and request a quiet room if necessary, Hamngatan 2, tel. 08/5413-0150, www.waxholmshotell.se, info@waxholmshotell.se). The hotel has a grill restaurant outside in summer and a fancy dining room inside.

Eating: Vaxholm's most tempting eatery, **$ Hembygdsgården ("Homestead Garden") Café** serves "summer lunches" (salads and sandwiches) and homemade sweets, with delightful outdoor seating around the Homestead Museum in Vaxholm's characteristic fishermen's quarter. Anette's lingonberry muffins are a treat (daily May-mid-Sept, closed off-season, tel. 08/5413-1980).

$ Boulangerie Waxholm is the perfect place for a *fika* break (coffee and sweets), but also serves sandwiches, salads, and hot dishes. From the south harbor (Söderhamnen), walk to the roundabout and turn left; you'll find it at the end of the block (Mon-Thu 6:30-18:30, Fri until 19:00, Sat-Sun from 8:00, tel. 08/5413-1872).

Grinda

The rustic, traffic-free isle of Grinda—half retreat, half resort—combines back-to-nature archipelago remoteness with easy proximity to Stockholm. The island is a tasteful gaggle of hotel buildings idyllically situated amid Swedish nature—walking paths, beaches, trees, and slabs of glacier-carved granite sloping into the sea. Since Grinda is a nature preserve (owned by the Stockholm Archipelago Foundation, or Skärgårdsstiftelsen), only a few families actually live here. There's no real town. But in the summer, Grinda becomes a magnet for day-trip-ping urbanites, which can make it quite crowded. Adding to its appeal is the nostalgia it holds for many Stockholmers, who fondly recall when this was a summer camp island. In a way, with red-and-white cottages bunny-hopping up its gentle hills and a stately old inn anchoring its center, it retains that vibe today.

Orientation to Grinda

Grinda is small and easy to manage. It's a little wider than a mile in each direction; you can walk from end to end in a half-hour. Its main settlement—the historic **Wärdshus building** (a busy hub of tourist activities including a restaurant, bar, Wi-Fi, and confer-ence facilities), hotel, and related amenities—sit next to its harbor, where private yachts and sailboats put in. Everything on the island is owned and operated by the same company; fortunately, it does a tasteful job of managing the place to keep the island's relaxing personality intact.

Major points of interest are well-signposted in Swedish: *Södra Bryggan* (south dock), *Norra Bryggan* (north dock), *Värdshus* (hotel at the heart of the island), *Gästhamn* (guest harbor); *Affär* (general store); *stuga/stugby* (cottage/s); *Grindastigen* (nature trail); and *Tält-plats* (campground).

TOURIST INFORMATION
The red cottage marked *Expedition/Lilla Längan* greets arriving visitors just up the hill from the Södra Grinda ferry dock. The staff answers questions, and the cottage serves as a small shop, a place to rent kayaks or saunas, and a reception desk for the island's cot-tages and hostel (open daily in season; Wärdshus general info tel. 08/5424-9491, www.grinda.se).

ARRIVAL IN GRINDA
Public ferries use one of two docks, at opposite ends of the island: Most use Södra Grinda to the south (nearest the hostel and cot-tages), while a few use Norra Grinda to the north (closer to the campground). From either of these, it's about a 10- to 15-minute walk to the action.

Sights in Grinda

Grinda is made to order for strolling through the woods, taking a dip, picnicking, and communing with Swedish nature. Watch the boats bob in the harbor and work on your Baltic tan. You can sim-ply stick to the gravel trails connecting the island's buildings, or for more nature, take the Grindastigen trail, which loops to the far end of the island and back in less than an hour (signposted from near the Wärdshus).

You can also rent a kayak or rent the private little sauna hut bobbing in the harbor. There's no bike rental here—and the island is a bit too small to keep a serious biker busy—but you could bring one on the boat from Stockholm.

As you stroll, you might spot a few haggard-looking tents through the trees. The right to pitch a tent here was established by the Swedish government during World War II, to give the downtrodden a cheap place to sleep. Those permissions are still valid, inherited, bought, and sold, which means that Grinda has a thriving community of tent-dwelling locals who camp out here all summer long (April-Oct). While some may be the descendants of those original hobos, these days they choose this lifestyle and live as strange little barnacles attached to Grinda. Once each summer they have a progressive tent-crawl bender before heading to the Wärdshus to blow a week's food budget on a fancy meal.

The island just across from the Södra Grinda dock (to the right) is Viggsö, where the members of ABBA have summer cottages and wrote many of their biggest hits.

Sleeping in Grinda

You have various options, in increasing order of rustic charm: hotel, hostel, and cottages. You can reserve any of these through the Wärdshus (tel. 08/5424-9491, www.grinda.se, info@grinda.se).

Grinda is busiest in the summer, when tourists fill its hotel; in spring and fall, it mostly hosts conferences. If sleeping at the hostel or cottages, arrange arrival details (you'll probably pick up your keys at the *Expedition/Lilla Längan* shed near the dock). The hostel and cottages charge extra for bed linens. If you have a tent, you can pitch it at the basic campsite near the north jetty for a small fee.

$$$$ Grinda Hotel rents 30 rooms (each named for a local bird or fish) in four buildings just above the Wärdshus. These are modern, comfortable, and made for relaxing, intentionally lacking distractions such as TVs or phones (cheaper if you skip breakfast; if dining at the restaurant, the "Wärdshus package" will save you a few kronor).

$ The 27 **cottages**—most near the Södra Grinda ferry dock—are rentable, offering a rustic retreat (kitchenettes but no running water, shared bathroom facilities outside). From mid-June to mid-August, these come with a one-week minimum and cost more.

¢ **Grinda Hostel** (Van-drarhem) is the place to sleep if you wish you'd gone to Swedish summer camp as a kid. The 44 bunks are in simple two- and four-bed cottages, surrounding a pair of fire pits (great shared kitchen/dining hall). A small pebbly beach and a basic sauna are nearby.

Eating in Grinda

All your options (aside from bringing your own picnic from Stockholm) are run by the hotel, with choices in each price range.

$$$$ Grinda Wärdshus, the inn at the center of the complex, has a good restaurant that combines rural island charm with fine food. You can choose between traditional Swedish meals and contemporary international dishes. Servings are small but thoughtfully designed to be delicious. Eat in the woody dining room or on the terrace out front (late June-Aug daily 12:00-24:00; weekends only—and some Fri—in off-season).

$$$ Grindas Framficka ("Grinda's Front Pocket") is a pleasant bistro that serves up basic but tasty food (seafood, salads, and pizza) right along the guest harbor. Order at the counter, then choose a table, or wait to be seated for a more formal atmosphere (early June-mid-Aug daily 11:00-22:00, otherwise sporadically open in good weather—especially weekends).

The **general store and café** (Lanthandel) just below the Wärdshus is the place to rustle up some picnic fixings. You'll also find coffee, ice cream, "one-time grills" for a disposable barbecue, and kayak rentals (open long hours daily early June-mid-Aug, Fri-Sun only in shoulder season).

Svartsö

The remote and lesser-known isle of Svartsö (svert-show, literally "Black Island"), a short hop beyond Grinda, is the "Back Door" option of the bunch. Unlike Grinda, Svartsö is home to a real community; islanders have their own school and library. But with only 80 year-round residents, the old generation had to specialize. Each person learned a skill to fill a niche in the community—one guy was a carpenter, the next was a plumber, the next was an electrician, and so on. While the island is less trampled than the others in this chapter (just one hotel and a great restaurant), it is reasonably well-served by ferries. Svartsö feels remote and potentially even boring for those who aren't wowed by simply strolling through meadows. But it's ideal for those who want to slow down and immerse themselves in nature.

Svartsö hosts the school for this part of the archipelago. Because Swedish law guarantees the right to education, even kids living on remote islands are transported to class. A school boat trundles from island to island each morning to collect kids headed for the school on Svartsö. If the weather is bad, a hovercraft retrieves them. If it's really bad, and all of the snow days have been used up, a helicopter takes the kids to school.

Orientation to Svartsö: The island, about five miles long and a half-mile wide, has four docks. The main one, at the southwestern tip, is called Alsvik (with the general store and restaurant). Halfway up is Skälvik, at the northeastern end is Söderboudd, and at the northwestern end is Norra Bryggan. Most boats stop at Alsvik, but if you want to go to a different dock, you can request a stop (ask the conductor on board, or use the semaphore signal at the dock).

At the **Alsvik dock,** the great little general store, called Svartsö Lanthandel, sells anything you could need and acts as the town TI, post office, pharmacy, and liquor store (daily mid-May-mid-Aug, more sporadic off-season but open year-round, tel. 08/5424-7325). You can rent bikes here; in busy times, call ahead to reserve (50 SEK/hour, 125 SEK/day). The little café on the dock sells drinks and light food, and rents $ cottages (bunk beds, shared outdoor toilets, tel. 08/5424-7110).

The island has a few paved lanes and almost no traffic. Residents own three-wheeled utility motorbikes for hauling things to and from the ferry landing. The interior consists of little more than trees. With an hour or so, you can bike across the island and back, enjoying the mellow landscape and chatting with the friendly big-city people who've found their perfect escape.

Eating in Svartsö: If you leave the Alsvik dock to the right and walk five minutes up the hill, you'll find the excellent **$$-$$$$ Svartsö Krog** restaurant. Run by Henrik, this place specializes in well-constructed, ingredient-driven dishes with local herbs and vegetables grown on the island and seafood caught by the local fishermen. Choose one of the three eating zones (each with the same menu): outside, upscale dining room, or original pub interior (an Old West-feeling tavern). Try the cod or "Svartsö-kebab" with homemade pita bread if available (daily lunch specials, 3- and 4-course fixed-price dinner menus, good wine and beer selection; lunch and dinner daily June-Aug; May and Sept dinner Fri-Sun, lunch Sat-Sun; closed Oct-April; tel. 08/5424-7255).

Sleeping in Svartsö: Away from the crowds, **$ Svartsö Skärgårdshotel och Vandrarhem** is a five-minute uphill walk from the Norra Bryggan dock (served by both Waxholmsbolaget and Cinderella Båtarna). The rooms are basic and include breakfast (bike rental available, 15-minute ride to Alsvik harbor and Svartsö Krog restaurant, open year-round, tel. 08/5424-7400, www.svartsonorra.se, info@svartsonorra.se).

Sandhamn

Out on the distant fringe of the archipelago—the last stop before Finland—sits the proud village of Sandhamn (on the island of Sandön). Literally "Sand Harbor," this is where the glacier got hung up and kept on churning away, grinding stone into sand. The town has a long history as an important and posh place. In 1897, the Royal Swedish Sailing Society built its clubhouse here, putting Sandhamn on the map as the yachting center of the Baltic—Sweden's answer to Nantucket. It remains an extremely popular stop for boaters—from wealthy yachties to sailboat racers—as well as visitors simply seeking a break from the big city.

The island of Sandön feels stranded on the edge of the archipelago, rather than immersed in it. Sandhamn is on its sheltered side. Though it's far from Stockholm, Sandhamn is very popular. During the peak of summer (mid-June through late August), it's extremely crowded. Expect to stand in line, and call ahead for restaurant reservations. But even during these times, the Old Town is relatively peaceful and pleasant to explore. If the weather's decent, shoulder season is delightful (though it can be busy on weekends).

Orientation to Sandhamn

You'll find two halves to Sandhamn: In the shadow of that still-standing iconic yacht clubhouse is a ritzy resort/party zone throbbing with big-money nautical types. But just a few steps away,

ARCHIPELAGO

around the harbor, is an idyllic time-warp Old Town of colorfully painted shiplap cottages tucked between tranquil pine groves. While most tourists come here for the resort, the quieter part of Sandhamn holds the real appeal.

Sandhamn has a summer-only **TI** (open June-mid-Aug) in the harbor area (www.destinationsandhamn.se.)

Sandhamn Walk

To get your bearings from the ferry dock, take this self-guided walk. Begin by facing out to sea.

As you look out to the little point across from the dock, notice the big yellow building. In the 18th century, this was built

as the **pilot house.** Because the archipelago is so treacherous to navigate—with its tens of thousands of islands and skerries, not to mention untold numbers of hidden underwater rocks—locals don't trust outsiders to bring their boats here. So passing ships unfamiliar with these waters were required to pick up a local captain (or "pilot") to take them safely all the way to Stockholm. The tradition continues today. The orange boats marked *pilot,* moored below the house, ferry loaner captains to oncoming ships. And, since this is the point of entry into Sweden, foreign ships can also be processed by customs here.

The little red shed just in front of the pilot house is home to a humble **town museum** that's open sporadically in the summer, featuring exhibits on Sandhamn's history and some seafaring tales.

Just above the barn, look for the yellow building with the blue letters spelling **Sandhamns Värdshus.** This traditional inn, built in the late 17th century, housed sailors while they waited here to set out to sea. During that time, Stockholm had few exports, so ships that brought and unloaded cargo there came to Sandhamn to load up their holds with its abundant sand as ballast. Today the inn still serves good food (see "Eating in Sandhamn," later).

Stretching to the left of the inn are the quaint storefronts of most of Sandhamn's **eateries** (those that aren't affiliated with the big hotel)—bakery, deli, and grocery store, all of them humble but just right for a simple bite or picnic shopping. Local merchants

ARCHIPELAGO

enjoy a pleasantly symbiotic relationship. Rather than try to compete with each other, they attempt to complement what the next shop sells—each one finding just the right niche.

The area stretching beyond these storefronts is Sandhamn's **Old Town**—a maze of wooden cottages that's an absolute delight to explore (and easily the best activity in town). Only 50 of Sandhamn's homes (of around 450) are occupied by year-rounders. The rest are summer cottages of wealthy Stockholmers, or bunkhouses for seasonal workers in the tourist industry. Most locals live at the farthest-flung (and therefore least desirable) locations. Imagine the impact of 100,000 annual visitors on this little town.

Where the jetty meets the island, notice (on the right) the old-fashioned telephone box with the fancy *Rikstelefon* logo. Just

to the right of the phone box, you can see the town's bulletin board, where locals post their classified ads. To the left at the base of the dock is Sandhamns Kiosk, a newsstand selling local and international publications (as well as candy and *mjukglass*—soft-serve ice cream). A bit farther to the left, the giant red building with the turret on top is the **yacht clubhouse** that put Sandhamn on the map, and still entertains the upper crust today with a hotel, several restaurants, spa, minigolf course, outdoor pool, and more. You'll see its proud SSS-plus-crown logo (standing for Svenska Segelsällskapet—Swedish Sailing Society) all over town. In the 1970s, the building was owned by a notorious mobster who made meth in the basement, then smuggled it out beneath the dock to sailboats moored in the harbor.

Look for the "Bluewater Oasis" **water station** in front of the yacht clubhouse. Due to Sandhamn's low groundwater level, and the enormous increase in visitors during summer months, local authorities impose water rationing part of the year. To provide more water, a filtration system was installed that purifies water direct from the Baltic Sea. It's totally drinkable, and a good place to fill up your water bottle.

Spinning a bit farther to the left, back to where you started, survey the island across the strait (Lökholmen). Just above the trees, notice the copper dome of an **observatory** that was built by this island's eccentric German oil-magnate owner in the early

20th century. He also built a small castle (not quite visible from here) for his kids to play in.

To stroll to another fine viewpoint, walk into town and turn left along the water. After about 50 yards, a sign on the right points up a narrow lane to *Posten*. This unassuming gravel path is actually one of Sandhamn's most important streets, with the post office, police department (which handles only paperwork—real crimes are deferred to the Stockholm PD), and doctor (who visits town every second Wednesday). While Sandhamn feels remote, it's served—like other archipelago communities—by a crack emergency-response network that can dispatch a medical boat or, in extreme cases, a helicopter. With top-notch hospitals in Stockholm just a 10-minute chopper ride away, locals figure that if you have an emergency here, you might just make it to the doctor faster than if you're trying to make it through congested city streets in an ambulance. At the end of this lane, notice the giant hill of the town's namesake sand.

Continuing along the main tree-lined harborfront strip, you can't miss the signs directing yachters to the *toalett* (toilet) and *sopor* (garbage dump). Then you'll pass the Sandhamns Guiderna office, a **travel agency** where you can rent bikes, kayaks, and fishing gear (tel. 08/640-8040). Just after that is the barn for the volunteer fire department (Brandstation). With all the wooden buildings in town, fire is a concern—one reason why Sandhamn restricts camping (and campfires).

Go beneath the skyway connecting the big red hotel to its modern annex. Then veer uphill (right) at the *Badstranden Trouville* sign, looking down at the minigolf course. After you crest the top of the hill, on the left is a big, flat expanse of rock nicknamed Dansberget ("Dancing Rock") because it once hosted community dances with a live orchestra. Walk out to enjoy fine **views** of the Baltic Sea—from here, boaters can set sail for Finland, Estonia, and

St. Petersburg, Russia. Looking out to the horizon, notice the three lighthouse towers poking up from the sea, used to guide ships to this gateway to the archipelago. The finish line for big boat races stretches across this gap (from the little house on the point to your left). In summer, this already busy town gets even more jammed with visitors, thanks to the frequent sailing races that end here. The biggest annual competition is the Götlandrunt, a round-trip from here to the island of Götland. In 2009, Sandhamn was proud to be one of just 10 checkpoints on the Volvo Ocean Race, a nine-month race around the world that called mostly at bigger cities (such as Boston, Singapore, and Rio).

Our walk is finished. You can head back into town. Or, to hit the beach, continue another 15 minutes to Trouville beach (explained next).

Sights in Sandhamn

Beaches (Stränder)

True to its name, Sandön ("Sandy Island") has some of the archipelago's rare sandy beaches. The closest, and local favorite, is the no-name beach tucked in a cove just behind the Old Town (walk through the community from the main boat dock, then follow the cove around to the little sandy stretch).

The most popular—which can be quite crowded in summer—is Trouville beach, at the opposite end of the island from Sandhamn (about a 20-minute walk). To find it, walk behind the big red hotel and take the right, uphill fork (marked with the low-profile *Badstranden Trouville* sign) to the "Dancing Rock," then proceed along the road. Take a left at the fork by the tennis courts, then walk about 10 minutes through a mysterious-feeling forest (sometimes filled with lingonberries and blueberries), until you reach a little settlement of red cottages. Take a right at the fork (look up for the *Till Stranden* sign), and then, soon after, follow the middle fork (along the plank walks) right to the beach zone: two swathes of sand marked off by rocks, stretching toward Finland.

Kvarnberget

Just inside the Old Town you'll find this little hilltop with a beautiful view of the sea. From the Sandhamns Värdshus B&B, take the path leading to the left and follow it straight past the old wooden houses until you see the hill. You can simply walk up the hill to enjoy the view, or pack a picnic (beware of seagulls hovering overhead, eager to steal your lunch).

Sleeping in Sandhamn

Sandhamn has a pair of very expensive top-end hotels, a basic but comfortable B&B, and little else. If you're sleeping on Sandhamn, the B&B is the best choice.

$$$$ Sands Hotell is a stylish splurge sitting proudly at the top of town. While oriented mostly to conferences and private parties, its 19 luxurious rooms also welcome commoners in the summer (elevator, spa, tel. 08/5715-3020, www.sandshotell.se, info@sandshotell.se).

$$$$ Sandhamns Seglarhotellet rents 79 nautical-themed rooms in a modern annex behind the old yacht club building (where you'll find the reception). The rooms are fine, but the prices are sky-high (loud music from disco inside the clubhouse—light sleepers should ask for a quieter back room, great gym and pool area, tel. 08/5745-0400, www.sandhamn.com, reception@sandhamn.com).

$ Sandhamns Värdshus B&B rents five rustic but tasteful, classically Swedish rooms in an old mission house buried deep in the colorful Old Town. To melt into Sandhamn and get away from the yachties, sleep here (mostly twins, all rooms share WC and shower, tiny cottage with its own bathroom for same price, includes breakfast, reception is at the restaurant—see next, tel. 08/5715-3051, www.sandhamns-vardshus.se, info@sandhamns-vardshus.se). The rooms are above a reception hall that is rented out for events, but after 22:00, quiet time kicks in.

Eating in Sandhamn

IN THE OLD TOWN

Sandhamn's most appealing eateries are along the Old Town side of the harbor.

$$-$$$$ Sandhamns Värdshus, right on the water, is the town's best eatery. They serve traditional Swedish food in three separate dining zones (which mostly share the same menu, but each also has its own specials): out on an inviting deck overlooking the water; upstairs in a salty dining room with views; or downstairs in a simple pub (daily lunch and dinner nearly year-round, lunch specials, tel. 08/5715-3051).

To grab a bite or assemble a picnic, browse through these smaller eateries: **$ Monrads Deli,** behind the yacht club, is a bright, innovative shop where you can buy sandwiches and salads, a wide array of meats for grilling, cheeses, cold cuts, drinks, fresh produce, and other high-quality picnic fixings (long hours daily in summer, mobile 0709-650-300).

In the opposite direction, **Westerbergs Livsmedel** grocery store has basic supplies (sporadic hours daily). **$$ Dykarbaren Café** serves lunches and dinners with indoor and outdoor seating (daily mid-June-mid-Aug, Wed-Sun only in shoulder season, closed off-season; tel. 08/5715-3554). **$ Ankaret** has a little market for takeaway and outdoor seating, serving smoked fish and shrimp, sandwiches, and ice cream. Just around the corner (uphill from the harbor and behind the Värdshus), **$ Sandhamns Bageriet** is a popular early-morning venue serving coffee, sweet rolls, and sandwiches (daily in summer, Sat-Sun only late-Aug-Sept).

AMONG THE YACHTIES

$-$$$$ Sandhamn Seglarhotell has several eateries, open to guests and nonguests. Out on the dock, about 100 yards to the right, is the posh Sea Club Poolbar and Grill, an American-style restaurant with outdoor tables surrounding a swimming pool (hamburgers and salads, open summer in good weather only). Upstairs in the building's main ballroom is an eatery serving good but pricey Swedish and international food (traditional daily lunch special). The restaurant enjoys fine sea views and has a bar/dance hall zone (with loud music until late, nearly nightly in summer). Down on the ground floor is a pub/nightclub (tel. 08/5745-0421).

ARCHIPELAGO

SOUTHEAST SWEDEN

Växjö • Glass Country • Kalmar • Öland Island

The sights in Sweden's southeastern province of Småland are a worthy runner-up to big-city Stockholm. More Americans came from this densely forested area than any other part of Scandinavia, and the House of Emigrants in Växjö tells the story well. Between Växjö and Kalmar is Glass Country, a 70-mile stretch of forest sparkling with glassworks that welcome guests to tour and shop. Historic Kalmar has a rare Old World ambience and the most magnificent medieval castle in Scandinavia. From Kalmar, you can cross one of Europe's longest bridges to hike through the limestone bedrock of the beachy island of Öland.

PLANNING YOUR TIME

While I'm not so hot on the Swedish countryside (OK, blame my Norwegian heritage), you can't see only Stockholm and say you've seen Sweden. Växjö and Kalmar give you the best possible dose of small-town Sweden. (I find Lund and Malmö, both popular side-trips from Copenhagen, relatively dull. And I'm not old or sedate enough to find a sleepy boat trip along the much-loved Göta Canal appealing.)

If you have the time and a car, the sights described in this section are an interesting way to spend a couple of days.

Without a car, or if you're short on time, I'd skip this area in favor of taking the direct, high-speed train from Copenhagen to Stockholm. Those with more time could spend a night in either Växjö or Kalmar, which can be reached by train.

By Car

Drivers can spend three days getting from Copenhagen to Stockholm this way:

Day 1: Leave Copenhagen after breakfast; drive over the bridge to Sweden and on to Växjö, touring Växjö's House of Emigrants; drive into Glass Country and tour one of the glassworks (I'd choose little Transjö Hytta or the Glass Factory) as well as the papermaking mill at Lessebo; arrive in Kalmar in time for dinner.

Day 2: Spend the day in Kalmar touring the castle and Kalmar County Museum, and browsing its people-friendly streets; if you're restless, cross the bridge for a joyride on the island of Öland, especially its south end.

Day 3: Start early for the five-hour drive north along the coast to Stockholm; break in Västervik, then stop in Söderköping for a picnic lunch and walk along the Göta Canal; continue driving north to Stockholm, arriving in time for dinner.

By Public Transit

Växjö and Kalmar are easy to visit by train. Without a car, I'd skip Glass Country and Öland, but if you wouldn't, take the bus (from Växjö to Kosta Boda glassworks, see "Växjö Connections," later).

Växjö

A pleasant, sleepy town of almost 85,000, Växjö (locals say VEK-hwuh; Stockholmers pronounce it VEK-shuh) is in the center of Småland. An important trading town for centuries, its name loosely means "where the road meets the lake." Coming in by train or car, you'd think it might mean "buried in a vast forest." Today an enjoyable three-mile path encircles that lake, and a farmers market enlivens the otherwise quiet main square on Wednesday and Saturday mornings.

My favorite activity in Växjö is to simply enjoy browsing through quintessential, small-town Sweden without a tourist in sight. While there isn't much heavy-duty sightseeing in Växjö, it does have a trio of worthwhile attractions: the earnest House of Emigrants, chronicling the plight of Swedes who fled to North America; the Smålands Museum, offering a convenient look at the region's famous glass without a trip to Glass Country; and the cathedral, decorated with fine modern glass sculptures.

In 1996, Växjö set itself the goal of becoming a fossil-fuel-free city by the year 2050. Now a single biomass power plant provides nearly all the community's heat and hot water, half of its energy comes from renewable sources, and carbon dioxide emissions are down considerably. Växjö earned the title "Greenest City in Europe" when it received the EU's first award for sustainable development in 2007.

Orientation to Växjö

Växjö's town center is compact and pedestrian-friendly; the train station, main square, and two important museums are all within two blocks of each other. Blocks here are short; everything I mention is within about a 15-minute walk of everything else. Tourists are so rare that a polite English-speaking visitor will find locals generous, warm, and helpful.

For a delightful three- or four-hour stopover, I'd do this loop from the station: Cross the tracks on the overpass to tour the glass and history museums (Smålands Museum and House of Emigrants). A block away is the lovely lake (encircled by a path), next to a pretty park and the cathedral. A block in front of the cathedral is the town square, Stortorget (with the TI); from there stretches the main commercial drag, Storgatan. Browse this orderly street before heading back to the station.

ARRIVAL IN VÄXJÖ

Växjö's modern train station has snack stands and coin-op lockers (an ATM is a block away to the right as you leave). Pick up a city map at the information desk. The station faces the heart of town; walk a few steps straight ahead, and you'll be in the pedestrian shopping zone. Everything in town is in front of you except the two main museums, which are behind the station; to reach these, cross the tracks using the pedestrian overpass. Drivers will find several parking lots near the station.

TOURIST INFORMATION

The **TI** is inside the municipal building facing the main town square, about a 10-minute walk from the train station. With your back to the station, go right two blocks to Kungsgatan, then left to the town square, a block away (June-Aug Mon-Fri 10:00-18:00, Sat until 14:00, closed Sun; shorter hours off-season; pick up Glass Country map and brochures here, Kronobergsgatan 6B, tel. 0470/733-280, www.vaxjoco.se).

Sights in Växjö

Växjö's attractions cluster around the north end of its pleasant lake and the surrounding park. The glass and history museums are on the hill just behind the train station (the pedestrian overpass takes you there).

Smålands Museum/Swedish Glass Museum (Sveriges Glasmuseum)

This instructive museum, while humble, celebrates the region of Småland and its glassmaking tradition. On the ground floor, the "Six Centuries of Swedish Glass" exhibit traces the history of the product that still powers the local economy. Upstairs you'll find more on glass, along with displays on the region's prehistory, and a look at Kronoberg County (which includes Växjö) in the 19th century. This is a handy place to learn a bit about glass if you're not headed deeper into Glass Country. Who knew that the person who designed the original Coca-Cola bottle in 1915 was a Swede?

Cost and Hours: 90-SEK combo-ticket includes House of Emigrants; June-Aug daily 10:00-17:00, shorter hours and closed

SOUTHEAST SWEDEN

Mon off-season; $ café with light meals, Södra Järnvägsgatan 2, tel. 0470/704-200, www.smalandsmuseum.se.

▲House of Emigrants (Utvandrarnas Hus)

If you have Swedish roots, this tidy museum is exciting. Even if you don't, it's an interesting stop for anyone with immigrant ancestors.

While modest, the well-presented, inspiring "Dream of America" exhibit captures the experiences of the more than one million Swedes who sought refuge in North America in the late 19th and early 20th centuries.

Cost and Hours: Same ticket and hours as Swedish Glass Museum; 50 yards down the hill behind the glass museum, Vilhelm Mobergs Gata 4, tel. 0470/20120, www.smalandsmuseum.se.

Visiting the Museum: As economic woes wracked Sweden from the 1850s to the 1920s, the country was caught up in an "American Fever." Nearly 1.3 million mostly poor Swedes endured long voyages and culture shock to seek prosperity and freedom in the American promised land. In that period, one in six Swedes went to live in the US. So many left the country that Swedish authorities were forced to rethink their social policies and to institute reforms.

The "Dream of America" exhibit focuses on various aspects of the immigrant experience. One display vividly recounts how 3.8 million new arrivals from around the world entered the US through Manhattan's Castle Garden processing center between 1886 and 1890. Firsthand accounts recall the entry procedure, including medical evaluations and an uncomfortable eye exam.

Swedes were compelled to emigrate in part because of the potato—a staple food in 19th-century Sweden. With dependable (or so everyone thought) nourishment, a peacetime king, and mandatory smallpox vaccinations, the mortality rate had been dropping even among ordinary Swedes. With good (or at least better) times, families got bigger. But as the sad model of a poor village demonstrates, when potato crops failed (especially from catastrophic freezes in 1867 and 1868), it wasn't possible to feed those extra mouths, and many Swedes were forced to leave.

They formed enclaves across North America: on farms and prairies, from New York to Texas, from Maine to Seattle—and, of course, in Chicago's "Swede Town" (the world's second-biggest Swedish town in 1900). The life-size *Snusgatan* re-creates the main street in a Swedish neighborhood—called "Snoose Boulevard," for

Swedish snuff. Other displays trace immigrant lifestyles, religion, treatment in the press, women's experiences, and the Swedish cultural societies that preserved the traditions of the Old World in the New. Rounding out the exhibit, homage is paid to prominent Swedish-Americans, including Charles Lindbergh and the second man on the moon, Buzz Aldrin.

Don't miss the display about the *Titanic,* which takes pains to point out that—after Americans—Swedes were the second-largest group to perish on that ill-fated vessel. On view are a few items that went to the bottom of the Atlantic with one of those Swedes.

The Moberg Room celebrates local writer Vilhelm Moberg (1898-1973), who put the Swedish immigrant experience on the map with his four-novel series *The Emigrants.* (These books—and two Max von Sydow/Liv Ullmann films based on them, *The Emigrants* and *The New Land*—are essential pretrip reading and viewing for Swedish-Americans.) Here you'll see a replica of Moberg's "writer's hut," his actual desk, and some original manuscripts.

Växjö Town Park (Växjö Stadspark)

Directly downhill from the House of Emigrants, you'll reach the big lake called **Växjösjön.** This is a fine place to relax with a picnic or go for a stroll. The pleasant three-mile park path around the lake takes you from manicured flower gardens through forested areas. The top part of the lake borders the inviting Linnéparken next to the cathedral (both described next).

A 10-minute walk around the top of the lake from the House of Emigrants is the town's modern **swimming hall** (*Simhall,* 80-SEK base price includes sauna; extra fee to tan, use the exercise room, or rent a towel or locker; family ticket available, call or check online for open-swim hours, tel. 0470/41204, www.medley.se/vaxjosimhall).

Växjö Cathedral (Växjö Domkyrka)

Växjö's striking orange church, with its distinctive double-needle steeple, features fine sacred art—in glass, of course. Its austere, bright-white interior is enlivened by gorgeous, colorful, and highly symbolic glass sculptures.

Cost and Hours: Free entry, daily 9:00-18:00.

Visiting the Cathedral: Near the entrance, pick up the brochure offering a detailed and evangelical self-guided tour. Near the back-left corner, the *Tree of Life and Knowledge* is a fantastically detailed candelabra. On one side, find Adam and Eve reaching for a very tempting apple with the clever snake egging them on from below. On the other side, Jesus and Mary welcome the faithful with arms outstretched. In similar opposition, the snake's tempting apple is suspended across from a bunch of grapes (symbolizing the wine of the Eucharist). At the front of the church, the modern stone altar stands before a glass-decorated triptych, itself a subtle interplay of light and dark. Explore the other pieces of glass art around the church, and take in its trio of pipe organs.

Linnaeus Park (Linnéparken)

This peaceful park beside the cathedral is dedicated to the great Swedish botanist Carl von Linné (a.k.a. Carolus Linnaeus). It has an arboretum, lots of well-categorized perennials, a cactus garden, and a children's playground.

▲Strolling Storgatan

Växjö's main pedestrian shopping boulevard offers a fun way to cap your visit. From the main square (with the TI), Storgatan stretches several blocks west. Walk the entire length of the street to observe small-town Sweden without any tourists. (You could make the popular Askelyckan bakery and café, at #24, your goal.) Imagine growing up or raising a family here: safe but boring, friendly but traditional, pleasant but predictable. The community seems super-content and super-conformist; it's very blond, with hints of multi-ethnicity. Feel the order and the quiet, like there's Valium in the air. Sweden is among the most highly taxed, affluent, and satisfied (and least church-going) societies in the world. This region lost more to emigration than any other, and it's thought-provoking to consider what impact that had on the character of those who remained behind (and their descendants).

Sleeping in Växjö

If you're parking a car in Växjö, be sure to use the pay-and-display meters. Parking is free from 18:00 until 9:00 the next morning.

$$$ PM & Vänner Hotel, with 74 stylish rooms, has a restful, in-the-know vibe. Extras include free loaner bikes, a gym, and a pool, which shares the rooftop with an appealing bar/terrace (elevator, sauna, pay parking, centrally located at Västergatan 10, tel. 0470/759-700, www.pmhotel.se, reservations@pmhotel.se).

$$ Elite Stadshotell is a big, modern, business-class hotel with all the comforts in its 163 rooms. It's conveniently set on the town's main square and close to everything (loaner bikes, about a block from the train station at Kungsgatan 6, tel. 0470/13400, www.elite.se, info.vaxjo@elite.se).

$ Hotell Värend is friendly, comfortable, and inexpensive. It has 24 worn but workable rooms at the edge of a residential neighborhood six blocks from the train station along Kungsgatan (elevator, free parking, a block beyond N. Esplanaden at Kungsgatan 27, tel. 0470/776-700, mobile 076-769-0700, www.hotellvarend.se, info@hotellvarend.se).

$$ Hotel Esplanad offers 26 comfortable, fresh rooms, all with private bath (free parking, N. Esplanaden #21A, tel. 0470/22580, www.hotellesplanad.com, info@hotellesplanad.com). From the train station, walk five blocks up Klostergatan and turn left on N. Esplanaden.

¢ Hostel: Växjö's fine **Vandrarhem Evedal Hostel** (an old resort hotel) is near a lake three miles north of town (breakfast extra, sheets extra, confirm reception hours before you arrive, tel. 0470/63070, www.vaxjovandrarhem.se, info@vaxjovandrarhem.se). From Växjö's train station, catch bus #7 (about hourly, 15 minutes).

Eating in Växjö

The restaurant scene is picking up in sleepy Växjö, with a few memorable spots in the center. If you're looking to save money, or if it's a Sunday—when other restaurants are closed—visit one of downtown Växjö's many Asian restaurants or kebab-and-pizza shops.

$$$$ PM & Vänner is a trendy eatery where a younger crowd stands in line to see and be seen. They have good international cuisine with Swedish flair, a mod black-and-white interior, and nice outdoor tables on the pedestrian mall. Their menu changes to feature seasonal and local ingredients (Mon-Sat 11:30-23:00, closed Sun, Storgatan 22 at corner of Västergatan, tel. 0470/759-711).

$$$$ Izakaya Moshi serves flavorful Japanese-style small plates (sushi, dumplings, salads, grilled fish, and meats) in an airy and light space. Choose from the long communal table, a cozy booth, or terrace seating when weather allows. Reservations are smart (Tue-Sat 17:00-21:00, closed Sun-Mon, immediately adjacent to the Smålands Museum at Södra Järnvägsgatan 2, tel. 0470/786-830, http://izakayamoshi.se).

$$$ Kafe De Luxe, about a block from the station, is a hip and funky hangout with live music many nights. They serve lunches and dinners daily—from burgers to *tarte flambée*—in a cozy Old World interior or under a happy tent outside (credit cards only, daily 11:30-24:00, Sandgärdsgatan 19, tel. 0470/740-409).

$$ Umami Monkey bills itself as having the "hippest burgers south of the North Pole"—and they just might be right. Their brioche-bun burgers pop with international flavors and come with great crispy fries (credit cards only, Mon-Fri 11:00-24:00, Sat from 12:00, closed Sun, Storgatan 18, tel. 0470/739-000).

$ Askelyckan Bakery Café, with an inviting terrace under a tree by a fountain on the city's main commercial drag, is a delightful place for a drink, cake, or light lunch on a sunny day (cakes, pastries, salads and sandwiches at lunch, daily 9:00-18:30, Storgatan 25, tel. 0470/12311).

Groceries: Visit the **ICA supermarket** at the corner of Sandgärdsgatan and Klostergatan, one block from the train station (long hours daily).

Växjö Connections

From Växjö by Bus to: Kosta (2-4/day, 1 hour, bus #218 from Växjö bus station; for schedules see www.lanstrafikenkron.se/en).

By Train to: Copenhagen (hourly, 2.5 hours), **Stockholm** (hourly, 3.5 hours, change in Alvesta, reservations required), **Kalmar** (hourly, 60-70 minutes). See the "Stockholm Connections" section in the Stockholm chapter for information on taking trains in Sweden.

Glass Country

Filling the remote-feeling woods between Växjö and Kalmar with busy glassmaking workshops, Sweden's famous Glasriket ("Kingdom of Crystal") is worth ▲▲ for those with a car. There's something deeply pleasing about a visit to a glassworks *(glasbruk):* Even at the bigger places—and especially at the smaller ones—you'll feel genuine artistic energy at work, as skilled craftspeople persuade glowing globs of molten glass to take shape.

The rich natural environment of this area, with inviting forests and lakes all around, has been fundamental to the glassworks (they needed a lot of wood to keep those fires going) and the region's other product, paper (small papermaking mills relied on plentiful water to wash cotton fiber to create paper pulp).

Visiting a glassworks is usually free and typically has two parts: a sales shop, which sells pieces produced on-site (and might have an exhibition of attractive pieces by local artists); and the hot shop, or *hytta,* where glassblowers are hard at work. At most glass-works, it's possible to walk through the hot shop—close enough to feel the heat from the glowing furnaces (arrive before the midafter-noon quitting time). Taking a guided tour of at least one hot shop is a must to really understand the whole process. (For starters, read the "Glassmaking in Sweden" sidebar.)

The glassworks listed here are a representative mix of the dozen or so you can visit in Glass Country, ranging from charming artistic workshops to big corporate factories. On the corporate side, Kosta Boda dominates; its flagship complex is the biggest of all the glassworks. But there are many smaller, independent producers, where you can get a more intimate view of the process.

Besides the tradition of hand-crafted glass, the region sustains the only surviving hand papermaking workshop in all of Scandina-via, in the town of Lessebo. It's well worth a visit.

For a complete change of pace, check out the local moose pop-ulation (you can visit them at the Moose and Farm Animal Park just outside Kosta).

Information: The *Glasriket/Kingdom of Crystal* maga-zine (available at any TI) and the region's official website (www.glasriket.se) describe the many glassworks that welcome the pub-lic. Most are open Mon-Fri 10:00-18:00, Sat until 16:00, and Sun 12:00-16:00—but there's plenty of seasonal variability. Check ahead to be sure the shop you want to visit will be open. The 100-SEK **Glasriket Pass** is worthwhile only if you're visiting several hot shops and doing some serious shopping (10 percent discount at certain shops once you've spent 700 SEK).

PLANNING YOUR TIME

Though you can take a bus from Växjö to Kosta (see "Växjö Con-nections"), the glassworks are realistically best reached with a car. Train travelers should instead take a careful look at the glass exhibit in Växjö's Smålands Museum, and then go straight to Kalmar.

By Car

With a car, the drive from Växjö to Kalmar is a 70-mile joy—light traffic with endless forest-and-lake scenery punctuated by numer-ous glassworks. The driving time between Växjö and Kosta is 45 minutes; it's another 45 minutes between Kosta and Kalmar.

Looking at a map, you'll notice the glassworks are scattered around the center of the region. While it would take the better part of a day to visit them all, distances are relatively short and roads are good. Still, it's smart to be selective. On a tight schedule, I'd visit the Glass Factory and Transjö Hytta, possibly Kosta and Bergdala, and the Lessebo paper mill, skipping the rest.

If you're visiting Glass Country en route from Växjö to Kal-

Glassmaking in Sweden

In the mid-16th century, King Gustav Vasa decided he wanted more fine glass to decorate his palace, so he invited German glassmakers to train his subjects, and the trend took off. It's no surprise that glassmaking caught on here in Sweden. The resources needed for glass are abundant: vast forests to fire the ovens, and lakes with an endless supply of sand. By the difficult 19th century—when a sixth of Sweden's population emigrated to North America—the iron mills had closed, leaving behind unemployed workers who were highly skilled at working with materials at high temperatures. Glassmaking was their salvation, and by the early 1900s, this region had more than 100 glassworks.

While glassmaking was important throughout Sweden, it was in the dense forest between Växjö and Kalmar that it took hold the strongest, and lasted the longest. When other materials became cheaper than glass (for example, paper cartons instead of glass bottles), the industry was hit hard, and it dried up in other parts of Sweden. But here in Glass Country, workers refocused their efforts: They still make some everyday items, but their emphasis is on high-quality art pieces that command top kronor. An Ikea wine glass made in China costs 10 SEK, while a handmade Swedish one might cost 150 SEK—but consumers interested in quality are willing to pay that premium.

The glassmaking process is fascinating—and hasn't changed much over the centuries. If you visit a hot shop, you'll see both everyday tableware and art pieces being created. "Mass-produced" tableware—such as wine glasses—is created by small teams of glassblowers who use an assembly-line system to produce a uniform product. Art-glass pieces, however, are never the same. The region has a passel of big-name designers, each with his or her own aesthetic and all considered local celebrities.

Either way, the process is the same. First, a worker places the

mar, consider this driving plan: Head southeast from Växjö on highway 25, following signs for *Kalmar*. To visit Bergdala, turn off after Hovmantorp; to skip it, head straight to Lessebo (and its paper mill). In Lessebo, turn north for Kosta and tour the big Kosta glassworks there. Then, detour slightly east to Orrefors and Orranäs Bruk, or head south on highway 28, watching for signs to *Transjö* for the best of the smaller, artsy glassworks. Pick up highway 25 again, where you'll soon see signs for the village of Boda

glassblowing rod into the furnace (notice the foot pedals used to open and close the doors) and grabs a blob of molten glass. Glassblowers have to move quickly—before the glass hardens too much—but deliberately, to avoid shattering the medium or burning their colleagues. After rolling the glass out on a heat-resistant graphite table to give it the desired shape, they blow into the end of the rod to open a space inside. If creating a mass-produced item, they generally stick it into a mold to ensure the correct dimensions. Other appendages are added; for example, if it's a wineglass with a stem and foot, separate pieces of glass are stretched out to the appropriate shape and attached.

For this entire process, the glass is at about 2,100 degrees Fahrenheit. If it gets too hot, glassblowers cool it down with water or air; if the glass needs to be reheated, they use a blowtorch or poke it momentarily back into the furnace. Finally, the area where the glass was attached to the rod is cut with an industrial diamond, broken off, and ground and polished smooth. When the piece is finished, it's set in a special oven to cool gradually.

At the workday's end, the raw materials for the next day's glass are dumped into giant, custom-made clay pots and placed in the ovens. Overnight, these will gradually melt down to the molten medium the glassblowers will need the next morning.

The last stop is quality control. Only the best pieces are deemed "first quality" *(1:A Sortering)*—you'll pay a premium for these flawless items. Some items, deemed "second quality" *(2:A Sortering),* have minor imperfections that bring the price down substantially. When shopping, pay close attention to these labels; if you don't need your glass perfect, you can save by looking for second quality.

SOUTHEAST SWEDEN

and its Glass Factory museum. From there, make a beeline east to Kalmar.

Sights in Glass Country

These attractions are tied together by the driving plan described above. Don't forget the historic paper mill, and the Moose and Farm Animal Park, described after the glassworks.

GLASSWORKS (GLASBRUKS)

These are listed in the order you'll reach them, from Växjö to Kalmar. Note that many workshops take a lunch break sometime between 11:00 and 12:00, and stop work entirely after about 15:00 or 15:30. Hours are always subject to change at the smaller glassworks, but they welcome a phone call to confirm open times. It's not uncommon for glassblowers to take vacation in July-Aug (along with the rest of Sweden).

▲Bergdala Glassworks (Bergdalahyttan)

The small, independent Bergdala glassworks, in a village of the same name, has an enjoyably artsy hot shop. Its well-stocked shop is full of its affordable trademark blue-rimmed glassware, and the engaging "museum" around back shows off a different sampling of local artists every year.

Cost and Hours: Free, gallery/shop open daily July-Aug 10:00-18:00 except Sat-Sun until 17:00, shorter hours off-season; glassblowing Mon-Fri 7:00-15:30 (lunch break 11:00-12:00); off highway #25 near Hovmantorp, tel. 0478/31650, http://bergdala-glastekniska-museum.se.

▲▲Kosta Boda

About an hour east of Växjö, the village of Kosta boasts the oldest of the *glasbruks,* dating back to 1742. Today, the Kosta Boda campus includes a modern outlet mall, a factory store, a fancy new art hotel...and, of course, the glassworks.

The highlight here is watching the **glassworks** in action. Visitors are welcomed to the hot-shop floor, where a team of glassblowers rotates through a carefully choreographed routine: grabbing a glob of molten glass on the blow pipe, rolling it on a steel table into a general shape, then turning and blowing the piece into its final form. You can visit the glassworks and its gallery on your own, but it's worth calling or emailing ahead to reserve a spot on a 30-minute English tour.

In the surprisingly modest **exhibition gallery,** each piece is identified with a photo and brief bio (in English) of its designer, which personalizes the art (often offered for sale).

Cost and Hours: Glassworks-free, usually open Mon-Fri 9:00-15:30 (lunch break 10:30-11:30), Sat-Sun 10:00-16:00; gallery-Mon-Fri 10:00-17:00, Sat-Sun until 16:00; www.kostaboda.se.

Tours: 100 SEK, usually 3/day in English, but best to arrange ahead by phone (tel. 0478/34529) or email (info@kostaboda.se).

Shopping: In the Kosta **factory outlet shop,** crystal "seconds" (with tiny bubbles or sets that don't quite match) and discontinued pieces are sold at good prices. This is duty-free shopping, and they'll happily mail your purchases home (Mon-Fri 10:00-18:00, Sat-Sun until 17:00). Don't confuse this with the big outlet mall across the street.

Sleeping and Eating: I ate well at the **cafeteria** inside the outlet mall, which features thrifty lunch specials. Nearby is the pricey **$$$$ Kosta Boda Art Hotel,** designed to impress. Everything's decorated to the hilt with (of course) artistic glass, created in the hot shop across the street. With Växjö and Kalmar so close, there's little reason to sleep here (tel. 0478/34830, www.kostabodaarthotel.se). But if you have a few extra minutes, poke around this over-the-top, world-of-glass complex, which includes a "glass bar," a mind-bending indoor swimming pool, and a restaurant where, on most evenings, you can watch an actual glassblower at work while you dine.

▲▲Transjö Hytta

Set up in an old converted farm 10 minutes south of Kosta, this tiny, friendly glassworks creates high-quality fine-art pieces. From the

main shop, a canal-like pond (enlivened with colorful glass art baubles) leads back to the hopping hot shop. Transjö—started by a pair of highly regarded glass designers—employs up-and-coming artists as apprentices, and their youthful vigor is infectious. You can feel the art oozing out of the ovens. The hot shop closes from July through December, but even if you don't catch the artists in action here, the setting is charming.

The gift shop out front sells a fine selection of one-of-a-kind glass art and limited-run production items made on-site (the *elevarbete*/apprentice works are cheaper). The shop keeps routine hours, but if you find it closed, dial the phone numbers posted on the door and someone will let you in.

Cost and Hours: Free, shop usually open early June-mid-Sept daily 9:00-17:00; hot shop hours irregular, closed July-Dec, smart to call or email ahead; tel. 0478/50700, www.transjohytta.com, info@transjohytta.com. To find it, look for *Transjö* signs just south of Kosta.

Orrefors and Orranäs Bruk

The town of Orrefors once had a glassworks with its own proud history, but glass is no longer commercially produced there. Formerly a premier art brand, Orrefors exists now only as a stepchild of Kosta Boda, and is mostly machine-made abroad. With its glassworks shuttered, Orrefors became a ghost town.

But concerned locals are blowing life back into Orrefors. Starting with an **open-air hot shop** that's already operating in a park near the old shop, their project will unfold in stages over several years, with the ultimate goal of reintroducing art-glass production to the town (to be sold under the name Orranäs Bruk).

Meanwhile, the town's dazzling **glass museum** continues to display its historic art pieces chronologically (from early-20th-century pieces with Art Nouveau flair through works from the 1940s).

Cost and Hours: Hot shop and glass museum July-Aug only; for the most current details, consult www.glasriket.se.

▲Glass Factory

Just off highway 25, in the little village of Boda, is a new enterprise, on the site of the former Boda glass production workshop. When glass producers fell on hard times in the 1980s and 1990s, many shops either folded or consolidated. When Boda closed, the municipality came together to buy its glass archive, an amazing record of artistic achievement that's now on display in the Glass Factory museum. There's also a great hot shop with regular demonstrations, a gallery of more modern Boda glass, and an affordable shop that sells glasswork from all over Scandinavia.

Cost and Hours: 60 SEK, late April-early Sept Mon-Fri 10:00-18:00, Sat-Sun 11:00-17:00; off-season Wed-Sun 11:00-17:00; in Boda at Storgotan 5, well-signed off highway 25, tel. 0471/249-360, www.theglassfactory.se.

OTHER ATTRACTIONS

▲▲Lessebo Handmade Paper Mill (Handpappersbruket)

The town of Lessebo has a 300-year-old paper mill (tucked next to a giant modern one) that's well worth a visit for its guided tour. Making handmade paper using strictly traditional methods (the newest piece of machinery is from the 1920s), Lessebo is a study in the way things used to be: Cotton fibers are soaked until they become pulp, packed into a frame, pressed, dried, glazed, and hand-torn into the perfect size and shape.

This paper has long been coveted throughout Sweden for special purposes: top-of-the-line stationery (for wedding invitations), impossible-to-forge embossed document paper (for certificates or important examinations), and long-lasting archival use (the cotton fibers ensure the paper will stay pristine for decades).

SOUTHEAST SWEDEN

You can visit the excellent gift shop on your own (watercolor paper, stationery, and cards), but to see papermaking in action, plan to join one of the fascinating 45-minute English tours. It's a rare opportunity to witness a centuries-old craft up close and personal.

Cost and Hours: Shop-June-Aug Mon-Fri 9:00-17:00, closed Sat-Sun, off-season closes at 16:00 and for lunch 12:00-13:00; 95-SEK guided tours depart 5/day in summer—check website for current times; look for black-and-white *Handpappersbruk* sign just after the Kosta turnoff, Storgatan 79, tel. 0478/47691, www. lessebopapper.se.

Grönåsen Moose and Farm Animal Park (Grönåsen Älg- & Lantdjurspark)

This offbeat attraction, just outside Kosta, demonstrates the love-hate relationship Swedes feel toward their moose population. A

third of a million of these giant, majestic beasts live in Sweden. They're popular with hunters but unpopular with drivers. At this attraction, you'll walk through the moose-happy gift shop before taking a mile-long stroll around the perimeter of a pen holding live moose. Periodic museum exhibits—life-size dioramas with stuffed moose (including one plastered to the hood of a car)—round out the attraction. You can even buy moose sausage to grill on-site. Sure it's a hokey roadside stop, and will hardly be a hit with animal-rights activists, but for many the park is an enjoyable stop.

Cost and Hours: 90 SEK, daily June-Aug 10:00-18:00, shorter hours April-May and Sept-Nov, closed off-season, just outside Kosta on the road to Orrefors, tel. 0478/50770, www.gronasen.se.

Eating in Glass Country

You'll find plenty of simple eateries designed for day-trippers. For example, the cafeteria in the outlet mall at the big Kosta complex is the perfect place for fast and cheap, Ikea-style Swedish grub.

If you'd like to linger over a more serious dinner, consider joining one of the special *hyttsill* **dinners** at various glass workshops. Traditionally, a hot shop's fires made it a popular place to convene after hours on frigid winter nights. People would huddle around the ovens and be entertained by wandering minstrel-type entertainers called *luffar*. The food was nothing special (*hyttsill* literally means "hot-shop herring," usually served with crispy pork, potatoes, and other stick-to-your-ribs fare), but it was a nice opportunity for a convivial rural community to get together. Today modern glassworks carry on the tradition, inviting tourists on several nights through the summer. They usually have live music and glassblowers working while you dine (figure around 400 SEK per person; for more information, see www.glasriket.se).

Kalmar

Kalmar feels like it used to be of strategic importance. In its heyday—back when the Sweden/Denmark border was just a few miles to the south—they called Kalmar Castle the "Key to Sweden." But today Denmark is distant, and Kalmar is a bustling small city of 64,000 (with 9,000 students in its university and maritime academy). Kalmar's salty old center, classic castle, and busy waterfront give it a wistful sailor's charm.

History students may remember Kalmar as the place where the treaty establishing the 1397 Kalmar Union was signed. This "three crowns" treaty united Norway, Sweden, and Denmark against their common enemy: German Hanseatic traders. It created a huge kingdom, dominated by Denmark, that lasted a bit more than a hundred years. But when the Swede Gustav Vasa came to power in 1523, Kalmar was rescued from the Danes, the union was dissolved...and even the European Union hasn't been able to reunify the Scandinavian Peninsula since.

Kalmar town was originally next to the castle. But that put the townsfolk directly in the line of attack whenever the castle was besieged. So, after a huge fire in 1647, they relocated the town on Kvarnholmen, an adjacent, easier-to-defend island. There it was encircled by giant 17th-century earthworks and bastions, parts of which still survive.

The town center of Kvarnholmen, the charming Old Town, the castle, and the nearby vacation island of Öland are all enjoyable to explore, making Kalmar Sweden's most appealing stop after Stockholm. Its tourist season is boom-or-bust, busiest from mid-June through mid-August.

Orientation to Kalmar

Kalmar is easily walkable and fun by bike. The mostly pedestrianized core of the town is on the island of Kvarnholmen, walled and with a grid street plan. The Old Town district is between Kvarnholmen and Kalmar Castle, which is on a little island of its own (a 10-minute walk from Kvarnholmen). The train station and TI sit on the edge of Kvarnholmen.

Additional islands make up Kalmar (including charming Ängö and mod Varvsholmen), but most visitors stick to Kvarnholmen, the Old Town, and the castle. If your time is limited, your top priorities should be a town walk, the castle, and the public beach just beyond the castle.

TOURIST INFORMATION

The TI is in the big, modern building next to the marina (summer Mon-Fri 9:00-18:00, Sat until 14:00, Sun closed; shorter hours off-season; Ölandskajen 9, tel. 0480/417-700, www.kalmar.com).

Ask about live music and entertainment; for example, there are often free concerts on Larmtorget, in Kvarnholmen, on Tue and Thu in the summer.

Biking: Many hotels have loaner or rental bikes for guests. Kalmar Cykeluthyrning (across from TI, closed Sun) rents bikes for 120 SEK per day (tel. 0480/010-600); Ölands Cykeluthyrning, with a convenient office right in the train station, has bikes for 140 SEK per day (handy one-way rentals with locations in Borgholm and Mörbylánga on Öland, daily late June-Aug 9:00-19:00, tel. 070/667-6280, www.olandscykeluthyrning.se). Consider riding the ferry from the harbor to the island of Öland (55 SEK—credit cards only, about hourly, 30 minutes, www.ressel.se), then renting a bike—Öland is made to order for a Swedish country bike ride. (Note you cannot ride a bike over the Öland Bridge.)

ARRIVAL IN KALMAR

Arriving at the combined train and bus station couldn't be easier (train ticket office open Mon-Fri 6:30-18:00, Sat until 15:00, Sun 10:30-17:00; lockers available). As you walk out the front door, the town center (Kvarnholmen) is dead ahead. The TI is 100 yards to your right, across the busy street on the harbor. Kalmar Castle and the Old Town are behind you (follow the tracks to your left until the first crosswalk, then follow the big tree-lined boulevard to the castle; with more time, take my scenic "Back-Streets Walk" to the castle, later).

Sights in Kalmar

▲▲ KALMAR CASTLE (KALMAR SLOTT)

This moated castle is one of Europe's great medieval experiences. The imposing exterior, anchored by stout watchtowers and cuddled by a lush park, houses a Renaissance palace interior. Built in the 12th century, the

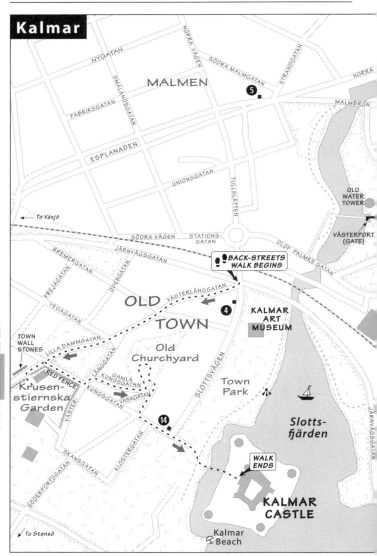

castle was enlarged and further fortified by the great King Gustav Vasa (r. 1523-1560) and lived in by two of his sons, Erik XIV and Johan III. In the 1570s, Johan III redecorated the castle in the trendy Renaissance style, giving it its present shape. Kalmar Castle remained a royal hub until 1658, when the Swedish frontier shifted south and the castle lost its strategic importance. Kalmar Castle was neglected, then used as a prison, distillery, and granary. Finally, in the mid-19th century, a newfound respect for history led to

Accommodations
1 Calmar Stadshotell
2 Frimurare Hotellet
3 Kalmar Sjömanshem Vandrarhem
4 Slottshotellet
5 Hotell Hilda
6 To Hotell Svanen

Eateries & Other
7 Källaren Kronan
8 Gröna Stugan
9 Bryggan
10 Grill Brygghuset
11 Kullzénska Caféet
12 Ernesto Restaurante
13 Supermarket
14 Söderport
15 Bike Rental (2)

the castle's renovation. Today, it's a vibrant sight giggling with kids' activities, park-like ramparts, and well-described historic rooms.

Cost and Hours: 135 SEK, daily late June-Aug 10:00-18:00, May-late June and Sept-Oct until 16:00; Nov-Dec Sat-Sun only 10:00-16:00, café and restaurant, tel. 0480/451-490, www. kalmarslott.se.

Tours: Catch the one-hour English tour to hear about the goofy medieval antics of Sweden's kings (included in admission, 3/day late June-mid-Aug—check website for current times).

Visiting the Castle: There's no designated route for visitors, but I've proposed one in the little tour below. Be sure to pick up and use the castle map to help you follow my route (castle rooms are not numbered except on the map—so the room numbers below refer to that handout). Otherwise, just read my tour in advance and then ramble, reading plaques as you go. There are good English descriptions throughout.

Approaching the castle, you'll cross a wooden drawbridge. Peering into the grassy, filled-in moat, look for sunbathers, who

enjoy soaking up rays while the ramparts protect them from cool winds. To play "king of the castle," scramble along these outer ramparts.

In the central **courtyard** is the canopied Dolphin Well, a fine work of Renaissance craftsmanship.

Access to most of the rooms is from the main courtyard, but we'll use the entrance just to the right of the gift shop (unceremoniously labeled *Toalett*).

Once inside, turn right to find the **Governor's Quarters** (Room 10) with a model of the early castle. Notice the bulky medieval shape of the towers, before they were capped by fancy Renaissance cupolas; and the Old Town that once huddled in the not-protective-enough shadow of the castle.

In the adjoining **Dungeon** (Room 9), you can peer down into the pit where unfortunate prisoners were held. The room was later converted into a kitchen (notice the big fireplace), and the pit became a handy place to dump kitchen waste.

Now go through the labyrinth of rooms to the right that show daily life at the castle: a reconstruction of the castle kitchen (Room 12), an excellent set of models showing the evolution of the building from medieval castle to Renaissance palace (Room 17), and an impressive copy of Erik XIV's 1561 coronation robe (Room 14, where there's also a complete rundown of the Vasa kings). In the next room (13) are similarly resplendent reproductions of royal gowns.

Now backtrack to where we entered, and climb the **Queen's Staircase** (Room 6), up steps made of Catholic gravestones. While this simply might have been an economical way to recycle building materials, some speculate that it was a symbolic move in support of King Gustav Vasa's Reformation, after the king broke with the pope in a Henry VIII-style power struggle.

At the top of the stairs, go left through the wooden door into the **Queen's Bedroom** (Room 23). The ornate 1625 Danish bed (captured from the Danes after a battle) is the only surviving original piece of furniture in the castle. The faces decorating the bed have had their noses chopped off, as superstitious castle-dwellers believed that potentially troublesome spirits settled in the noses. This bed could easily be disassembled ("like an Ikea bed," as my guide put it) and moved from place to place—handy for medieval kings and queens, who were forever traveling throughout their realm. Smaller servants' quarters adjoin this room.

Proceed into the **Checkered Hall** (Room 24). Examine the intricately inlaid wall panels, which make use of 17 different types of wood—each a slightly different hue. Appreciate the faded Renaissance frescoes throughout the palace.

Continue into the **dining room** (a.k.a. Gray Hall—Room 25) for the frescoes of Samson and Delilah high on the wall. The table is set for an Easter feast (based on a detailed account by a German visitor to one particular Easter meal held here). For this holiday event, the whole family was in town—including Gustav Vasa's two sons, Erik XIV and Johan III. Erik's wife, Katarzyna Jagiellonka, was a Polish Catholic (their marriage united Sweden, Poland, and Lithuania into a grand empire); for her, Easter meant an end to Lenten abstinences. Notice the diverse savories on the table, including fish patties with egg, elaborate pies, and chopped pike in the shape of pears. The giant birds are for decoration, not for eating. Logically, forks (which resembled the devil's pitchfork) were not used—just spoons, knives, and hands.

The door in the far corner with the faded sun above it leads to the **King's Chamber** (Room 26). Notice the elaborate lock on the door, installed by King Erik XIV because of constant squabbles about succession. The hunting scenes inside have been restored a bit too colorfully, but the picture of Hercules over the left window is original—likely painted by Erik himself. Examine more of the inlaid panels. To see the king's toilet, peek into the little room to the left of the fireplace, with a fine castle illustration embedded in its hidden door (if closed, ask a museum wench to open it). Also in here was a secret escape hatch the king could use in case of trouble. Perhaps King Erik XIV was right to be so paranoid; he eventually died under mysterious circumstances, perhaps poisoned by his brother Johan III, who succeeded him as king.

Backtrack through the dining room and continue into the **Golden Hall** (Room 27), with its gorgeously carved (and painstakingly restored) gilded ceiling. The entire ceiling is suspended

from the true ceiling by chains. If you visually trace the lines of the ceiling, the room seems crooked—but it's actually an optical illusion to disguise the fact that it's not perfectly square. Ponder the portraits of the royal family: Gustav Vasa, one of his wives, sons Erik XIV and Johan III, and Johan's son Sigismund. Imagine the reality-show-level dysfunction that carbonated the social scene here back then.

Peek into **Agda's Chamber** (Room 28), the bedroom of Erik's consort. The replica furniture re-creates how it looked when the king's kept woman lived here. Later, the same room was used for a different type of captivity: as a prison cell for female inmates.

Cut across to the top of the King's Staircase (also made of gravestones like the Queen's Staircase, and topped by a pair of lions). The big door leads to the grand **Green Hall** (Room 31), once used for banquets and now for concerts.

At the end of this hall, the **chapel** (Room 32) is one of Sweden's most popular wedding venues (up to four ceremonies each

Saturday). As reflected by the language of the posted Bible quotations, the sexes sat separately: men, on the warmer right side, were more literate and could read Latin; women, on the cooler left side, read Swedish. The fancy pews at the front were reserved for the king and queen.

Going through the door to the right of the altar, you'll enter a stairwell (Room 33), above which hangs a model ship, donated by a thankful sailor who survived a storm. In the next room (34) is Anita, a taxidermic horse who served with the Swedish military (until 1937).

The rest of the castle complex includes the vast **Burnt Hall** (Room 36), where in summer you'll likely find an interesting special art exhibit.

▲THE OLD TOWN

The original Kalmar town burned (in 1647) and is long gone. But the cute, garden-filled residential zone that now fills the parklike space between the castle and the modern town center is worth a look.

It's a toy village of colorfully painted wooden homes, tidy yards, and perfect picket fences. Locals still call it the Old Town

(Gamla Stan), even though almost everything here is newer
than the buildings on Kvarnholmen, now the heart of town.

Back-Streets Walk to the Castle

Consider a slight detour strolling through the Old Town on
your way from the train station to the castle (the walk is marked on
the "Kalmar" map). Begin where the pleasant, tree-shaded Slotts-
vägen boulevard intersects with little Västerlånggatan, the cobbled
street angling to the right.

Västerlånggatan: Wandering down this quaint lane, enjoy
the time-passed cottages as you peek over fences into private gardens. You'll pass behind the grand mansion (now the recommended **Slottshotellet**) that belonged to the prestigious Jeansson family,
who donated the parkland near the castle to the town.

Continue through the first intersection, following the path
through the middle of the grassy park. As you cross the road on the
far side of the park, you'll pass two lines of stones, a small surviving
remnant of Kalmar's town wall (on the right).

Krusenstiernska Gården: Watch on the left for the entrance
to this relaxed, kid-friendly garden, with its breezy café selling
traditional homemade cakes. Poke inside to discover a manicured
world of charming plantings clustered around a well, and peek
into time-warp workshops. On summer evenings, this garden is
a venue for top Swedish comedy acts, which pack the place (park
free, daily 11:00-18:00 in summer, shorter hours on weekends and
off-season).

From the garden, backtrack to the street and follow the red
fence to the right. Where the fence ends, jog left and squeeze between the yellow and red houses.

Gamla Kungsgatan and the Old Churchyard: Immerse
yourself in this Swedish village world of charming cottages and
flower-filled window boxes. At the bottom of the lane, on the left,
watch for the Old Churchyard (Gamla Kyrkogården), dating from
the 13th century and scattered with headstones. It's virtually all
that remains of the original Old Town. Look for the monument
topped by a statue of a man carrying a boy (St. Christopher, patron
of traders and seafarers). Circling this slab, you'll see the floor plan
of the original cathedral, an image looking down the cathedral's
nave, and a rendering of the town before it was destroyed. The cathedral tower—which had partially survived the 1647 fire—was
torn down in 1678 by the Swedes themselves, who wanted to en-

sure that their enemies (the Danes) couldn't use the tower to launch an attack on the castle.

About 50 yards farther into the yard, the stone slab on the pedestal (marked *Kalmarunionen 600 år*) commemorates the 600th anniversary of the 1397 Kalmar Union, which united the Nordic states. On June 14, 1997, the contemporary leaders of those same nations—Sweden, Norway, Denmark, Finland, and Iceland— came here to honor that union. You can see their signatures etched in the stone.

Exit the churchyard the way you came in, turn right on the paved street, and take the first left (down Kungsgatan) to the main boulevard. You'll be facing the town park and the castle; on your left is the appealing, recommended Söderportcafé (with an inviting terrace and an economical buffet-lunch deal).

Town Park (Stadsparken): Unfurling along the waterfront between the castle and the city, this beautifully landscaped arboretum-style garden is Kalmar's playground. While thoughtfully planned, it's also rugged, with surprises around each corner. Locals brag that their region is a "banana belt" that enjoys a milder climate than most of Sweden; some of the plants here grow nowhere else in the country. This diversity of foliage, and the many sculptures and monuments, make the park a delight to explore. The modern art museum stands in an appropriately modern building in the center of the park.

▲Kalmar Beach (Kalmarsundsbadet)

Kalmar's best beach is at the edge of the Old Town, just beyond the castle. On a hot summer day, this is a festive and happy slice of Swedish life—well worth a stroll even if you're not "going to the beach." With snack stands, showers, sand castles, wheelchair beach access, and views of the castle and the island of Öland, the beach has put Kalmar on the fun-in-the-sun map. It's quite popular with RVers and the yachting crowd. And if you enjoy people-watching, it's a combination Swedish beauty pageant/tattoo show. For some extra views and kid-leaping action, be sure to walk to the end of the long pier.

The beach stretches a mile south. Beyond it is the charming little seafront community of **Stensö,** with its own pocket-size harbor and charming fishing cottages.

▲KVARNHOLMEN TOWN CENTER

Today, downtown Kalmar is on the island of Kvarnholmen. Get your bearings with the following walk, which basically just cuts straight through the length of town. Then dig into its museums.

Kvarnholmen Self-Guided Walk

Most action centers on the lively, restaurant-and-café-lined square called **Larmtorget,** a few steps uphill from the train station. This is the most inviting square in town for outdoor dining—scout your options for dinner later tonight. It's also the nightlife center of town, especially on Tuesday and Thursday evenings in summer, when there are often free concerts. The many cafés bordering the square are a remind-

er that this is a college town, with lots of students; and a tourist town, with lots of vacationing Swedes. The fountain depicts David standing triumphantly over the slain Goliath—a thinly veiled allusion to King Gustav Vasa, who defeated the Danes (the fountain's reliefs depict his arrival in Kalmar in 1520).

The area just to the north, up Larmgatan, is a charming old quarter with the historic Västerport gate and a restored old water tower. The tower, dating from 1900, was turned into a modern apartment building, winning an award for the architect who successfully maintained the tower's historic design.

But for now, we'll stroll straight through town on the main pedestrian shopping street, **Storgatan** (with Ben & Jerry's on the corner). Kvarnholmen is a planned Renaissance town, laid out on a regular grid plan (after the devastating 1647 fire consumed the Old Town). While a 1960s push to "modernize" stripped away much of the Old World character, surviving historic buildings and the lack of traffic on most of its central streets make Kvarnholmen a delightful place to stroll.

The first major cross-street, Kaggensgatan, leads (to the right, past a fine row of 17th-century stone houses) down to the harbor; a block to the left, on the right (at #26), is the landmark and recommended Kullzénska Caféet, whose owners refused to let this charming 18th-century merchant's house be torn down to make way for "progress." (It remains a good place for *fika* in a genteel setting.)

Continue window-shopping your way down Storgatan. On the right just after #20, admire the building marked *1667,* with the cannonballs decorating the doorway. This was the home of a war profiteer—a lucrative business in this military-minded town (now an inviting gift shop with local products, teas, chocolates, and cheese).

Storgatan leads to the town's main square, **Stortorget.** Built in the 17th century in a grand style befitting a European power, the "big square" tries a little too hard to show off—today it feels too big and too quiet (locals prefer hanging out on the cozier Larmtorget).

The **cathedral** *(domkyrkan)* dominating the square is the biggest and (some say) finest Baroque church in Sweden. Its interior,

which contains a gigantic 17th-century pulpit and bells from the earlier town cathedral, has been elegantly restored to its original glory. Its architect was inspired by the great Renaissance churches of Rome. The interior is all very high-church (for such a Lutheran country), with a fine Baroque altar, carved tombstones used for flooring, and homogeneous white walls (free, Mon-Fri 8:00-20:00, Sat-Sun from 9:00, shorter hours off-season, free noon "Lunch Music" organ concerts daily in summer—check the program on the board left of the entrance). Facing the cathedral is the decorated facade of the **Town Hall** *(rådhuset).*

From here, go straight through the square and stroll down Storgatan. Notice the fine old houses, all lovingly cared for. At the end of town, the area beyond Östra Vallgatan (the old eastern wall of the city) has a pleasant **park** and small **swimming beach.** You may notice dads out with their babies—most Scandinavians get over a year of paid leave for the mom and dad to split as they like. (They're nicknamed "Latte Dads," and cafés complain that they clog their floor space with too many carriages.)

Head across the street and down the stairs toward the playground (to the left) to find, on a little pier in the water, the last remaining *klapphus*—laundry building—in Kalmar (and Scandinavia). In the mid-1800s, four of these small, wooden structures with floating floors stood here at the sea-side. Washers would stand in barrels inset around the central laundry pool for a better working position. Today the *klapphus* is still occasionally used for washing rugs and carpets. The Baltic seawater is considered good for carpet health.

Across the water is the island neighborhood of Varvsholmen, which once housed an eyesore shipyard but has been converted into a futuristic residential development. To the left of Varvsholmen is the sleepy island neighborhood of Ängö, traditionally home to sailors and fishermen, now one of Kalmar's most desirable residential areas. To the right stretches the Öland Bridge. When built in 1972 to connect Öland with the mainland, it was Europe's longest bridge.

• *Your walk is finished. Hooking around to the right, you first reach the former city bathhouse (in a 1909 Art Nouveau building), which faces the tiny Kalmar Maritime Museum (described later). A block beyond that, the waterfront is dominated by giant red-brick buildings—steam mills once used to grind flour. Today this complex houses the fascinating Kalmar County Museum, described next.*

▲▲Kalmar County Museum (Kalmar Läns Museum)

This museum is worth a visit for its excellent exhibit on the royal ship *Kronan*, a shipwrecked 17th-century warship that still sits on the bottom of the Baltic just off the island of Öland. Soggy bits and rusted pieces, well-described in English, give visitors a here's-the-buried-treasure thrill. It's a more intimate look at life at sea than Stockholm's grander Vasa Museum, though this exhibit lacks the boat's actual hull. (The amateur marine archaeologist Anders Franzén was instrumental in locating and salvaging both ships.)

Cost and Hours: 120 SEK, daily 10:00-17:00, off-season until 16:00, included 45-minute English tours daily in season at 13:00; kid-friendly café on floor 4, Skeppsbrogatan 51, tel. 0480/451-300 www.kalmarlansmuseum.se.

Visiting the Museum: While the museum has plenty of exhibits, your visit will focus mostly on the third floor with the *Kronan* shipwreck artifacts.

Beyond the entry, the first floor has temporary exhibits and shows off the cannons recovered from the *Kronan* wreckage. In those days, cannons were so valuable they were prized the way a Rolls Royce would be today, so each one has its own story (described in English). In the years following the ship's sinking, these cannons were the only artifacts considered worth recovering.

From the first floor, I'd skip the temporary exhibits on Floor 2 and head directly to Floor 3, which displays salvage from the *Kronan*. Twice the size of Stockholm's famous *Vasa*, this warship was a floating palace and the most heavily armed vessel in the world. But it exploded and sank about three miles beyond the island of Öland in 1676. The painted wall at the elevator shows the dramatic event: The *Kronan*'s admiral misjudged conditions and harnessed too much wind, causing the vessel to tip and its gun ports to fill with water. As the ship began to list into the water, a fallen lantern ignited explosives in the hold, and...BLAM! The ship went right down. Its Danish and Dutch foes—who hadn't fired a shot—happily watched it sink into the deep. Of the 850 people on board, only about 40 were rescued. The wreck's whereabouts were forgotten until 1980, when it was rediscovered by the same oceanographer who found the *Vasa*.

Head into the exhibit, where you'll view a model of the shipwreck site (press the button for a short English explanation). You'll see a cross-section of the mighty vessel and a recovered carving of the potbellied Swedish king (one of many such carvings that decorated the ship). The small theater plays a 15-minute film about the ship (English subtitles).

The replica of the middle gun deck leads to the exhibit's most interesting section, which explains everyday life on board. The 850 sailors who manned the ship (about the population of a midsized town of that age) represented all walks of life, "all in the same boat." Engaging illustrations, eyewitness accounts, and actual salvage items bring the story to life. You'll see guns, musical instruments, a medicine chest, dishes, and clothing—items that emphasize the nautical lifestyles of the simple, common people who worked and perished on the ship. A treasure chest contains coins from all around the known world at the time, each one carefully identified.

The final exhibit (with another short film) reminds us that the *Kronan* still rests on the sea floor, awaiting funding to be raised to the surface. You'll see a replica of the diving bell used in 1680 to retrieve the cannons, and the modern diving bell from very early explorations of the site. Today a dedicated crew of scientists and enthusiasts—including, at times, Sweden's King Carl XVI Gustav—continue to dive to recover bits and pieces.

For extra credit, head up to Floor 4 for its exhibit on **Jenny Nyström,** an early-1900s Kalmar artist who gained fame for her cute Christmas illustrations featuring elves and pixies. You'll see some of her children's books and textbooks, as well as some less commercial, more artistic portraits (with a touch of Art Nouveau flair). Ponder Nyström's status as a proto-feminist icon: She was one of the first female artists to support her family by selling her paintings.

Kalmar Maritime Museum (Kalmar Sjöfartsmuseum)

This humble, dusty little exhibit sits a long block beyond the Kalmar County Museum. It's a jumble of photos of vessels, model boats, charts, and other seafaring bric-a-brac that traces the nautical story of Kalmar up to modern times. The collection is displayed in four rooms of a former apartment, shuffled between beautiful porcelain stoves left behind by a previous owner. (These were display models for his stove retail business.) While it's explained by an English booklet (that you can borrow or buy), the volunteers love to talk and are eager to show you around.

Cost and Hours: 50 SEK, daily mid-June-Aug 11:00-16:00, off-season Sun only 12:00-16:00, Södra Långgatan 81, tel. 0480/15875, www.kalmarsjofartsmuseum.se.

Sleeping in Kalmar

IN KVARNHOLMEN TOWN CENTER

$$$ Calmar Stadshotell is a 132-room fancy hotel filling its 1907 historic shell right on Kalmar's main square, Stortorget (elevator, Stortorget 14, tel. 0480/496-900, www.profilhotels.se, calmarstadshotell@profilhotels.se).

$$ Frimurare Hotellet, in a grand old building overlooking inviting Larmtorget square, is just steps from the train station.

Warmly run, the place has soul and a disarmingly friendly staff. Rich public areas, wide-plank hardwood floors, and chandeliers give it a 19th-century elegance. Guests can help themselves to coffee, tea, juice, and other refreshments in the lounge anytime. The 35 rooms provide modern comfort amid period decor. Because it's squeezed between a café-packed square and a park that's popular for concerts, it can come with some noise (RS%, elevator, free sauna, a few loaner bikes free for Rick Steves readers, 50 yards in front of train station, Larmtorget 2, tel. 0480/15230, www.frimurarehotellet.se, info@frimurarehotellet.se).

$ Kalmar Sjömanshem Vandrarhem, a charming green house built in 1910 for sailors and now used for student housing, opens to travelers in the summer (mid-June-mid-Aug only). While its 13 rooms are very simple and bathrooms are down the hall, it has an inviting TV lounge, handy guest kitchen, and a peaceful garden behind a white picket fence facing the harbor (family rooms, sheets and towels extra, no breakfast, plenty of nearby pay parking, Ölandsgatan 45, tel. 0480/10810, www.kalmarsjomanshem.se, info@kalmarsjomanshem.se).

OUTSIDE THE TOWN CENTER

$$$ Slottshotellet ("Castle Hotel") is an enticing splurge in the atmospheric Old Town. It's the nicely upgraded but still homey former mansion of a local big shot. The 70 rooms—some in the mansion, others sprinkled throughout nearby buildings—sit across a leafy boulevard from Kalmar's Town Park, just up the street from the castle (Slottsvägen 7, tel. 0480/88260, www.slottshotellet.se, info@slottshotellet.se).

$$ Hotell Hilda has 12 good rooms in an updated old house, located in a modern residential zone just over the canal from the town center (elevator, limited free parking—reserve a spot when you book, Esplanaden 33, tel. 0480/54700, www.hotellhilda.se, info@hotellhilda.se). The ground-floor Kallskänken café, which doubles as the reception, serves good salads and sandwiches (Mon-Sat 8:00-21:00, Sun 10:00-20:00; if checking in outside of these times, email for the door code).

¢-$$ Hotell Svanen, a 15-minute walk or short bus ride from the center in the Ängö neighborhood, has a mix of nicer hotel rooms with private bath, cheaper rooms with shower down the hall, and hostel beds (no more than six beds per room). Services include laundry and kitchen facilities, a TV room, a sauna, and rental bikes and canoes. While it's a bit institutional, you can't argue with the value (family rooms, sheets extra in hostel rooms, breakfast extra; reception daily 7:30-21:00, elevator, Rappegatan 1, tel. 0480/25560, www.hotellsvanen.se, info@hotellsvanen.se). You'll see a blue-and-white hotel sign and a hostel symbol at the edge of town on Ängöleden street, a mile from the train station. Catch bus #405 at the station to Ängöleden (2-3/hour, 5 minutes), or take a taxi for about 70 SEK.

Eating in Kalmar

Kalmar has a surprising number of good dining options for a small city. For lunch, look for a *dagens rätt* (daily special), which gets you a main dish, salad, bread, and usually coffee or a soft drink.

IN KVARNHOLMEN TOWN CENTER

$$$ Källaren Kronan, open only for dinner, is a candlelit cellar restaurant with romantic tables under low stone arches. They serve old-time Swedish dishes, including elk, as well as modern cuisine (nightly 18:00-23:00, Ölandsgatan 7, tel. 0480/411-400).

$$$$ Gröna Stugan ("The Green Cottage") has a great location just off the harbor. Enjoy the eclectic menu (burgers, short ribs, grilled arctic char) on their patio deck or in the light and bright dining room. Reservations are smart (lunch Mon-Fri 11:30-14:00, dinner Mon-Sat 17:00-22:00, closed Sun, Larmgatan 1, tel. 0480/15858, www.gronastuganikalmar.se).

$$$ Bryggan sits inside the Baronen shopping mall, but it's poised over the harbor with view tables inside and deck seating over the water. They serve typical bistro fare, including burgers and fish-and-chips (Mon-Sat 10:00-19:00, Sat until 16:00, Sun 11:00-16:00, tel. 0480/363-626).

$$ Grill Brygghuset, open only in summer, seems made to order for visiting yachters. Casual and right on the dock, it grills everything, serving traditional and modern dishes with local ingredients (mid-June-mid-Aug Tue-Sun from 17:00, closed Mon, at the marina near the TI and train station at Ölandskajen 9, tel. 073-354-0333).

$$ Kullzénska Caféet, a cozy, antique-filled eatery in a historic 18th-century house, is great for a *fika* break. They serve sandwiches and homemade pastries, but locals adore the always-fresh berry cobblers (with vanilla sauce or ice cream). While it has street seating, the dining rooms upstairs are what it's all about (Mon-Fri 10:00-18:30, Sat-Sun 12:00-16:00, on the second floor at Kaggensgatan 26, at the corner of Norra Långgatan, tel. 0480/28882).

$$ Ernesto Restaurante is driven by Ernesto, who came here from Naples 30 years ago. This local favorite for pasta and pizza has a high-energy feel with good indoor and outdoor seating (most menu items available for takeout, great selection of Italian wines, daily from 16:00, Södra Långgatan 5, tel. 0480/24100).

Supermarket: The **Co-op** has everything you need for a good picnic, including a salad bar (daily 6:00-23:00, in the Baronen shopping mall at the harbor, on Skeppsbrogatan).

NEAR THE CASTLE

The castle lawn cries out for a picnic (buy one at the Co-op supermarket before your visit). Or you can grab a bite in the café inside the castle itself. Otherwise, consider:

$$$$ Söderport, just across the street from the castle, offers an all-you-can-eat buffet, as well as a regular menu; the dining room is pleasantly spacious but the outdoor patio has castle views (daily 11:30-15:00 & 17:00-22:00, Slottsvägen 1, tel. 0480/12501). There's live music Wed-Sat evenings.

Kalmar Connections

From Kalmar by Train to: Växjö (hourly, 60-70 minutes), **Copenhagen** and its airport (hourly, 4 hours, some transfer in Alvesta), **Stockholm** (almost hourly, 4.5-5 hours, transfer in Alvesta, reservations required; some prefer the slower but more scenic coastal route via Linköping).

By Bus to Stockholm: The bus to Stockholm is much cheaper but slower than the train (3/day, fewer on weekends, 6 hours).

ROUTE TIPS FOR DRIVERS

Kalmar to Stockholm (230 miles, 5 hours): Leaving Kalmar, follow *E-22 Lindsdal* and *Nörrköping* signs. Sweden did a cheap widening job, paving the shoulders of the old two-lane road to get

3.8 lanes. Fortunately, traffic is polite and sparse. There's little to see, so stock the pantry, set the compass on north, and home in on Stockholm. Make two pleasant stops along the way: Västervik and the Göta Canal.

Västervik is 90 miles north of Kalmar, with an 18th-century core of wooden houses (3 miles off the highway, *Centrum* signs lead you to the harbor). Park on the waterfront near the great little smoked-fish market (Mon-Sat).

Sweden's famous **Göta Canal** consists of 190 miles of canals that cut the country in half, with 58 locks *(slussen)* that work up to a summit of 300 feet. It was built 150 years ago at a low ebb in the country's self-esteem—with more than seven million 12-hour man-days (60,000 men working about 22 years)—to show her industrial might. Today it's a lazy three- or four-day tour, which shows Sweden's zest for good living.

Take just a peek at the Göta Canal over lunch, in the medieval town of **Söderköping**: Stay on E-22 past where you'd think you'd exit for the town center, then turn right at the *Kanalbåtarna/Slussen*. Look for the *Kanal P* signs leading to a handy canalside parking lot. From there, walk along the canal into the action. The TI on Söderköping's Rådhustorget (a square about a block off the canal) has good town and Stockholm maps, a walking brochure, and canal information (www.ostergotland.info). On the canal is the Kanalbutiquen, a yachters' laundry, shower, shop, and WC, with idyllic picnic grounds just above the lock. From the lock, stairs lead up to the Utsiktsplats pavilion (commanding view).

From Söderköping, E-22 takes you to Nörrköping. Follow *E-4* signs through Nörrköping, past a handy rest stop, and into Stockholm. The *Centrum* is clearly marked.

Öland Island

The island of Öland—90 miles long and only 8 miles wide—is a pleasant resort known for its windmills, wildflowers, dry-stacked limestone walls, happy birdwatchers, prehistoric sights, roadside produce stands on the honor system, and Swede-filled beaches. This castaway island, with only about 25,000 permanent residents, attracts some 2.5 million visitors annually. It's a top summer vacation destination for Swedes—even the king and queen have their summer home here. Because of its relatively low rents, better weather, and easy bridge access to the mainland, Öland is also a popular bedroom community for Kalmar. If you've got a car, good weather, and some time to spare—and if the place isn't choked with summer crowds—Öland is a fine destination, especially if you don't rush it. (For a basic map of Öland, see the "Southeast Sweden" map at the beginning of this chapter.)

Dubbed the "Island of Sun and Wind," Öland enjoys a steady sea breeze and an even warmer climate than already mild Kalmar (remember, "warm" is relative in Sweden). And, because its top layer of soil was scraped off by receding glaciers, it has a completely different landscape than the pines-and-lakes feel of mainland Sweden. The island's chalky limestone plain, rich soil, and lush vegetation make it feel almost more Midwestern US than Baltic (Öland is one of Sweden's premier agricultural zones). Visitors are pleasantly surprised by the island's colorful spring wildflowers and bright sunshine, which works its magic on both holidaymakers and artists.

Centuries ago, the entire island was the king's private hunting ground. Because local famers were not allowed to fell trees (and there are fewer here than on the mainland), they made their simple houses from limestone. The island's 34 limestone churches, which were also used for defense, have few windows. Limestone walls demarcate property and contained grazing livestock.

When built in 1972, the **Öland Bridge** from Kalmar to the island was Europe's longest (3.7 miles). The channel between Kalmar and Öland is filled with underwater rocks, making passage here extremely treacherous—but ideal for the Vikings' flat-bottomed boats. (In fact, "Kalmar" comes from the phrase "stones in water.") The little town of Färjestaden, near the island end of the bridge, was once the "ferry town" where everyone came and went; today it sits sad and neglected.

GETTING THERE

The island is most worthwhile if you have a car and at least four extra hours to explore. **Drivers** simply head north from Kalmar a few minutes on highway 137 to the Öland Bridge. Once across, highway 136 is the island's main north-south artery. **Buses** regularly connect Kalmar with the town of Borgholm (56 SEK, nearly hourly in summer, 50-60 minutes) and, with less frequency, to other Öland destinations (check www.klt.se). **Bikers** with adequate time enjoy biking to and around Öland, but note that you're not allowed to ride your bike on the bridge; instead, take the ferry that carries bikers across from Kalmar to Öland (55 SEK, about hourly, 30 minutes, www.ressel.se). To plan a bike trip, consult with Ölands Cykeluthyrning, who will rent you a bike in either Kalmar, Borgholm, or Mörbylånga and let you return it at a different location (shops in Kalmar and on the island in Borgholm and Mörbylånga, tel. 076-103-9879, www.olandscykeluthyrning.se).

Sights on Öland

Visitors can (and do) spend days exploring this giant island's plea-
sures. But on a quick visit of a few hours, you'll want to narrow your
focus. Your basic choices are center/north Öland (developed and
resorty, with royal sights, and more services—and traffic) or south
Öland (rugged, remote, and scenic, with tilting windmills, charming cottages, and a giant limestone plain dominating its middle;
demands more time). I've outlined a few basic ideas for each area
below, but these are just the beginning—there's much more to discover on Öland.

Regardless if you go north or south, make your first stop just
after crossing the bridge at Öland's mid-island **TI** in Färjestaden—
follow signs off the bridge for *turistbyrå* (Träffpunkt Öland 102,
tel. 0485/88800, www.olandsturist.se; there's also a branch on the
main street in Borgholm). Friendly staff can help you plan a reasonable agenda for the amount of time you have.

CENTRAL/NORTH ÖLAND

For a quick spin to the island, stick with the strip of Öland just
north of the bridge. As you drive north along highway 136, keep
an eye out for some of Öland's characteristic, old-fashioned windmills. Occasional stone churches dot the landscape (including the
one in Räpplinge—just off the main road—where the royals wor-
ship when in town).

The island's main town is **Borgholm** (BOY-holm), about a
30-minute drive north of the bridge. Borgholm itself isn't much to
see, unless you enjoy watching Swedes at play. It's got a smattering
of turn-of-the-century wooden villas, erected here after the royal
palace was built nearby. Notice that many of these have a humble
shack in the garden: Locals would move into these cottages so they
could rent the main villas to vacationing Stockholmers in the summer and make a killing. The traffic-free main drag, Storgatan, is
lined with tacky tourist shops and ice-cream parlors (Ölandsglass,
at #10, is tops). There's also a handy **TI** right on the town's main
street.

A pair of interesting sights sits on the hill just above Borgholm (to reach them, you can either drive or hike—get details at
TI). **Borgholm Castle** (Borgholms Slott), which looks like Kalmar
Castle with its top blown off, broods on the bluff above town, as
if to remind visitors of the island's onetime strategic function. Its
hard-fought history has left it as the empty shell you see today—
impressive, but not worth the entry fee (www.borgholmsslott.se).

From near the castle, you can hike down to a more recent and
appealing royal sight, the current royal summer residence, **Solliden Palace** (Sollidens Slott). It was built in 1906 in an Italianate

style after physicians to Queen Victoria suggested the milder Öland climate might ease her ill health. The palace interior is off-limits, but its sprawling, gorgeously landscaped garden is open to us common-ers. Divided into Italian

(geometrical and regimented), English (wild), and Dutch (flowers) sections, the Solliden garden complex is well worth a wander (105 SEK, daily 11:00-18:00, last entry at 17:00, closed off-season, on-site café, tel. 0485/15356, www.sollidensslott.se).

SOUTH ÖLAND

A 60-mile loop south of the bridge will give you a good dose of the island's more remote, windy rural charm. Head south on highway 136 to experience the savannah-like limestone plain, old grave-yards, and mysterious prehistoric monuments. Just before the town of Karlevi you'll notice the beautifully preserved stone mill to your right, the **Karlevi Stenkvarn.** While its weathervane shows the year 1791, no one is really sure how old it is (it's a Dutch-type mill that was common in the 19th century). Island farmers milled flour here until the mid-1950s.

Near here, you have a few choices for getting a closer look at the limestone plain: Either take the road (heading east) that starts near the town of Resmo, or drive on a little farther to the turnoff just past N. Bårby. This open, agricultural landscape (quite unlike the forested mainland) was first farmed during the Stone Age, and still shows evidence of how the land was divided among farmers in medieval days.

Gettlinge Gravfält (off the road about 10 miles up from the south tip, just south of Smedby) is a wonderfully situated, boat-shaped, Iron Age graveyard littered with monoliths and overseen by a couple of creaky old windmills. It offers a commanding view of the windy and mostly treeless island.

Farther south is the **Eketorp Prehistoric Fort** (Eketorps Borg), a reconstructed fifth-century stone fort that, as Iron Age

forts go, is fairly interesting. Several evocative huts and buildings are designed in what someone imagined was the style back then, and the huge rock fort is surrounded by runty Linderöd pigs, a native breed that was common in Sweden 1,500 years ago. A sign reads: "For your convenience and pleasure, don't leave your children alone with the animals" (120 SEK, daily mid-June-mid-Aug 10:30-18:00, closed off-season, tel. 0485/662-000, www.eketorp.se). It's near the southern tip of the island, on the eastern side: When you approach Grön-högen on the main road from the north, look for signs on the left.

You can push on even farther to the very southern tip of the island, home to Sweden's tallest lighthouse, the **Ottenby Nature Center** (exhibits on the nature and culture of the island), and the **Ottenby Bird Observatory,** where ornithologists monitor migratory birds that pass through this major flyway (guided tours available, see www.birdlife.se).

PRACTICALITIES

This section covers just the basics on traveling in this region (for much more information, see *Rick Steves Scandinavia*). You'll find free advice on specific topics at www.ricksteves.com/tips.

MONEY

In Scandinavia, credit cards are widely accepted, even for small purchases. In Sweden cash is rarely used; you can't pay for a tram, metro, or bus ride with cash in Stockholm, for example. If you must have cash, Sweden uses the Swedish kronor (SEK): 1 SEK equals about $0.13. To roughly convert prices in kroner to dollars, divide prices by eight (100 SEK = about $12.50). Check www.oanda.com for the latest exchange rates.

The standard way for travelers to get kronor is to withdraw money from an ATM using a debit card, ideally with a Visa or MasterCard logo. Before departing, call your bank or credit-card company: Confirm that your card(s) will work overseas, ask about international transaction fees, and alert them that you'll be making withdrawals in Europe. Also ask for the PIN number for your credit card—you may need it for Europe's "chip-and-PIN" payment machines (see below; allow time for your bank to mail your PIN to you). To keep your valuables safe while traveling, wear a money belt.

Dealing with "Chip and PIN": Most credit and debit cards now have chips that authenticate and secure transactions. European cardholders insert their chip card into the payment slot, then enter a PIN. (Until recently, most US cards required a signature.) Any American card with a chip will work at Europe's hotels, restaurants, and shops—although sometimes the clerk may ask for a signature. But some self-service payment machines—such as those at train stations, toll roads, or unattended gas pumps—may not accept your card, even if you know the PIN. If your card won't work, look for a cashier who can process the transaction manually—or pay in cash.

Dynamic Currency Conversion: If merchants or hoteliers offer to convert your purchase price into dollars (called dynamic currency conversion, or DCC), refuse this "service." You'll pay more in fees for the expensive convenience of seeing your charge in dollars. If an ATM offers to "lock in" or "guarantee" your conversion rate, choose "proceed without conversion." Other prompts might state, "You can be charged in dollars: Press YES for dollars, NO for kronor." Always choose the local currency.

STAYING CONNECTED

The simplest solution is to bring your own device—mobile phone, tablet, or laptop—and use it just as you would at home (following the tips below, such as connecting to free Wi-Fi whenever possible).

To call Sweden from a US or Canadian number: Whether you're phoning from a landline, your own mobile phone, or a Skype account, you're making an international call. Dial 011-46 and then the area code (minus its initial zero) and local number. (The 011 is our international access code, and 46 is Sweden's country code.) If dialing from a mobile phone, you can enter + in place of the international access code—press and hold the 0 key.

To call Sweden from a European country: Dial 00-46 followed the area code (minus its initial zero) and local number. (The 00 is Europe's international access code.)

To call within Sweden: If you're dialing within an area code, just dial the local number; but if you're calling outside your area code, you have to dial both the area code (which starts with a 0) and the local number.

To call from Sweden to another country: Dial 00 followed by the country code (for example, 1 for the US or Canada), then the area code and number. If you're calling European countries with phone numbers that begin with 0, you'll usually have to omit that 0 when you dial.

Tips: If you bring your own mobile phone, consider signing up for an international plan; most providers offer a global calling plan that cuts the per-minute cost of phone calls and texts, and a flat-fee data plan.

Use Wi-Fi whenever possible. Most hotels and many cafés offer free Wi-Fi, and you'll likely also find it at tourist information offices (TIs), major museums, and public-transit hubs. With Wi-Fi you make free or inexpensive domestic and international calls via a calling app such as Skype, FaceTime, or Google+ Hangouts.

Sleep Code

Hotels are classified based on the average price of a typical en suite double room with breakfast in high season.

$$$$	**Splurge:**	Most rooms over 2,000 SEK
$$$	**Pricier:**	1,500-2,000 SEK
$$	**Moderate:**	1,000-1,500 SEK
$	**Budget:**	500-1,500 SEK
¢	**Hostel/Backpacker:**	Under 500 SEK
RS%	**Rick Steves discount**	

Unless otherwise noted, credit cards are accepted, and free Wi-Fi is available. Comparison-shop by checking prices at several hotels (on each hotel's own website, on a booking site, or by email). For the best deal, always book directly with the hotel. Ask for a discount if paying in cash; if the listing includes **RS%**, request a Rick Steves discount.

When you can't find Wi-Fi, you can use your cellular network to connect to the Internet, send texts, or make voice calls. When you're done, avoid further charges by manually switching off "data roaming" or "cellular data."

Without a mobile device, you can make calls from your hotel and get online using public computers (there's usually one in your hotel lobby or at local libraries). Most hotels charge a high fee for international calls—ask for rates before you dial. For more on phoning, see www.ricksteves.com/phoning. For a one-hour talk on "Traveling with a Mobile Device," see www.ricksteves.com/travel-talks.

SLEEPING

I've categorized my recommended accommodations based on price, indicated with a dollar-sign rating (see sidebar). I recommend reserving rooms in advance, particularly during peak season. Once your dates are set, check the specific price for your preferred stay at several hotels. You can do this either by comparing prices on sites such as Hotels.com or Booking.com, or by checking the hotels' own websites. To get the best deal, contact my family-run hotels directly by phone or email. When you go direct, the owner avoids any third-party commission, giving them wiggle room to offer you a discount, a nicer room, or free breakfast. If you prefer to book online or are considering a hotel chain, it's to your advantage to use the hotel's website.

For complicated requests, send an email with the following information: number and type of rooms; number of nights; arrival date; departure date; and any special requests. Use the European style for writing dates: day/month/year. Hoteliers typically ask for your credit-card number as a deposit. In general, hotel prices can soften if you do any of the following: offer to pay cash, stay at least three nights, or travel off-season.

Even though most hotels in Sweden base their prices on demand, it is possible to find lower prices during the summer and on weekends. Check hotel websites for deals. To find an apartment or room in a private home, try Airbnb, Booking.com, and the HomeAway family of sites (HomeAway, VRBO, and VacationRentals).

EATING

I've categorized my recommended eateries based on price, indicated with a dollar-sign rating (see sidebar).

Restaurants are often expensive. Alternate between picnics (outside or in your hotel or hostel); cheap, forgettable, but filling cafeteria or fast-food fare ($20 per person); and atmospheric, carefully chosen restaurants popular with locals ($40 per person and up). Ethnic eateries—Turkish, Greek, Italian, and Asian—offer a good value and a break from Swedish food.

If you want to enjoy a combination of picnics and restaurant meals on your trip, you'll save money by eating in restaurants at lunch (when there's usually a daily special—*dagens rätt*—and food is generally cheaper), then picnicking for dinner.

The *smörgåsbord* is a revered Scandinavian culinary tradition. Seek it out at least once during your visit. Begin with the fish dishes, along with boiled potatoes and *knäckebröd* (Swedish crisp bread). Then move on to salads, egg dishes, and various cold cuts. Next it's meatball time! Pour on some gravy as well as a spoonful of lingonberry sauce. Still hungry? Make a point to sample the Nordic cheeses and the racks of traditional desserts, cakes, and custards.

Hotel breakfasts are a huge and filling buffet, generally included but occasionally a $15-or-so option. It usually features fruit, cereal, various milks, breads, crackers, cold cuts, pickled herring, caviar paste, and boiled eggs. The brown cheese with the texture of earwax and a slightly sweet taste is called *gede ost* ("goat cheese"); Swedes prefer a spreadable variety called *messmör*.

In Sweden, most alcohol is sold only at state-run liquor stores called Systembolaget (though weak beer is available at supermarkets). To avoid extremely high restaurant prices for alcohol, many Swedes—and tourists—buy their wine, beer, or spirits at a store and then drink at a public square; this is illegal although often done. One local specialty is *akvavit*, a strong, vodka-like spirit distilled from potatoes and flavored with anise, caraway, or other herbs and spices—then drunk ice-cold. *Lakka* is a syrupy-sweet liqueur made from cloudberries, the small orange berries grown in the Arctic.

Restaurant Price Code

I've assigned each eatery a price category, based on the average cost of a typical main course. Drinks, desserts, and splurge items (steak and seafood) can raise the price considerably.

$$$$ **Splurge:** Most main courses over 200 SEK

$$$ **Pricier:** 150-200 SEK

$$ **Moderate:** 100-150 SEK

$ **Budget:** Under 100 SEK

In Sweden, a hot dog stand or other takeout spot is **$**; a sit-down café is **$$**; a casual but more upscale restaurant is **$$$**; and a swanky splurge is **$$$$**.

Service: Good service is relaxed (slow to an American). When you want the bill, say, *"Kan jag få notan, tack."* Throughout Sweden, a service charge is included in your bill, so there's no need to leave an additional tip. In fancier restaurants or any restaurant where you enjoy great service, round up the bill (about 5-10 percent of the total check).

TRANSPORTATION

By Train and Bus: Trains cover many Scandinavian destinations. If you're traveling beyond Stockholm and want to see if a rail pass could save you money, check www.ricksteves.com/rail. If you're buying tickets as you go, note that prices can fluctuate. To research train schedules and fares, visit the Swedish train website: www.sj.se. Nearly any long-distance train ride requires you to make a reservation before boarding (the day before is usually fine).

Don't overlook long-distance buses (e.g., between Stockholm and Oslo), which are usually slower than trains but have considerably cheaper and more predictable fares. Sweden's biggest bus carrier is Swebus (www.swebusexpress.se).

By Car: It's cheaper to arrange most car rentals from the US. For tips on your insurance options, see www.ricksteves.com/cdw, and for route planning, consult www.viamichelin.com. Bring your driver's license. Local road etiquette is similar to that in the US. Ask your car-rental company about the rules of the road, or check the US State Department website (www.travel.state.gov, select "International Travel," then "Country Information," then search for your destination and click "Traffic Safety and Road Conditions"). Use your headlights day and night; it's required in most of Scandinavia. A car is a worthless headache in Stockholm—there's a congestion tax to enter the city center on weekdays. If you must drive into the city, park it safely (get tips from your hotelier). You'll encounter one-way tolls of up to €60 on major bridges including the Øresund Bridge between Sweden and Denmark and the Svinesund Bridge between Sweden and Norway.

By Boat: Boats are romantic, scenic, and sometimes the most efficient—or only—way to link destinations in coastal Sweden. Advance reservations are recommended when using overnight boats in summer or on weekends to link Stockholm with Helsinki (www.vikingline.fi and www.tallinksilja.com). For cruising the nearby islands, see the Stockholm's Archipelago chapter.

By Plane: SAS is the region's dominant airline (www.flysas. com). Well-known cheapo airlines EasyJet (www.easyjet.com) and Ryanair (www.ryanair.com) fly into Scandinavia.

HELPFUL HINTS

Emergency Help: To summon the **police** or an **ambulance**, dial 112. For passport problems, call the **US Embassy** (in Stockholm: passport services by appointment only, info tel. 08/783-5375, emergency tel. 08/783-5300, https://se.usembassy.gov).

If you have a minor illness, do as the locals do and go to a pharmacist for advice. Or ask at your hotel for help—they'll know of the nearest medical and emergency services. For other concerns, get advice from your hotelier.

Theft or Loss: To replace a passport, you'll need to go in person to an embassy (see above). Cancel and replace your credit and debit cards by calling these 24-hour US numbers collect: Visa—tel. 303/967-1096, MasterCard—tel. 636/722-7111, American Express—tel. 336/393-1111. In Sweden, to make a collect call to the US, dial 020-799-111; press zero or stay on the line for an operator. File a police report either on the spot or within a day or two; you'll need it to submit an insurance claim for lost or stolen rail passes or electronics, and it can help with replacing your passport or credit and debit cards. Precautionary measures can minimize the effects of loss—back up your photos and other files frequently. For more information, see www.ricksteves.com/help.

Time: Europe uses the 24-hour clock. It's the same through 12:00 noon, then keep going: 13:00, 14:00, and so on. Sweden, like most of continental Europe, is six/nine hours ahead of the East/ West Coasts of the US.

Holidays and Festivals: Europe celebrates many holidays, which can close sights and attract crowds (book hotel rooms ahead). For more on holidays and festivals in Sweden, check the Scandinavia Tourist Board website: www.goscandinavia.com. For a simple list showing major—though not all—events, see www. ricksteves.com/festivals.

Numbers and Stumblers: What Americans call the second floor of a building is the first floor in Europe. Europeans write dates as day/month/year, so Christmas 2020 is 25/12/20. Commas are decimal points and vice versa—a dollar and a half is 1,50, and there are 5.280 feet in a mile. Europe uses the metric system: A kilogram is 2.2 pounds; a liter is about a quart; and a kilometer is six-tenths of a mile.

RESOURCES FROM RICK STEVES

This Snapshot guide is excerpted from the latest edition of *Rick Steves Scandinavia,* which is one of many titles in my ever-expanding series of guidebooks on European travel. I also produce a public television series, *Rick Steves' Europe,* and a public radio show, *Travel with Rick Steves.* My website, www.ricksteves.com, offers free travel information, a forum for travelers' comments, guidebook updates, my travel blog, an online travel store, and information on European rail passes and our tours of Europe. If you're bringing a mobile device on your trip, you can download my Rick Steves Audio Europe app, featuring dozens of self-guided audio tours of the top sights in Europe and travel interviews about Europe. You can get Rick Steves Audio Europe via Apple's App Store, Google Play, or the Amazon Appstore. For more information, see www.ricksteves.com/audioeurope. You can also follow me on Facebook and Twitter.

ADDITIONAL RESOURCES

Tourist Information: www.goscandinavia.com
Passports and Red Tape: www.travel.state.gov
Packing List: www.ricksteves.com/packing
Travel Insurance: www.ricksteves.com/insurance
Cheap Flights: www.kayak.com or www.google.com/flights
Airplane Carry-on Restrictions: www.tsa.gov
Updates for This Book: www.ricksteves.com/update

HOW WAS YOUR TRIP?

If you'd like to share your tips, concerns, and discoveries after using this book, please fill out the survey at www.ricksteves.com/feedback. Thanks in advance—it helps a lot.

INDEX

Explore Europe

At ricksteves.com you can browse through thousands of articles, videos, photos and radio interviews, plus find a wealth of money-saving travel tips for planning your dream trip. And with our mobile-friendly website, you can easily access all this great travel information anywhere you go.

TV Shows

Preview the places you'll visit by watching entire half-hour episodes of Rick Steves' Europe (choose from all 100 shows) on-demand, for free.

your travel dreams into affordable reality

Radio Interviews

Enjoy ready access to Rick's vast library of radio interviews covering travel

tips and cultural insights that relate specifically to your Europe travel plans.

Travel Forums

Learn, ask, share! Our online community of savvy travelers is a great resource

for first-time travelers to Europe, as well as seasoned pros. You'll find forums on each country, plus travel tips and restaurant/hotel reviews. You can even ask one of our well-traveled staff to chime in with an opinion.

Travel News

Subscribe to our free Travel News e-newsletter, and get monthly updates from Rick on what's happening in Europe.

Audio Europe™

Gear up for your next adventure at ricksteves.com

Light Luggage

Pack light and right with Rick Steves' affordable, custom-designed rolling carry-on bags, backpacks, day packs and shoulder bags.

Accessories

From packing cubes to moneybelts and beyond, Rick has personally selected the travel goodies that will help your trip go smoother.

Experience maximum Europe

Save time and energy

This guidebook is your independent-travel toolkit. But for all it delivers, it's still up to you to devote the time and energy it takes to manage the preparation and logistics that are essential for a happy trip. If that's a hassle, there's a solution.

Rick Steves Tours

A Rick Steves tour takes you to Europe's most interesting places with great

guides and small groups of 28 or less. We follow Rick's favorite itineraries, ride in comfy buses, stay in family-run hotels, and bring you intimately

close to the Europe you've traveled so far to see. Most importantly, we take away the logistical headaches so you can focus on the fun.

travelers—nearly half of them repeat customers—along with us on four dozen different itineraries, from Ireland to Italy to Athens. Is a Rick Steves tour the right fit for your travel dreams? Find out at ricksteves.com, where you can also request Rick's latest tour catalog. Europe is best experienced with happy travel partners. We hope you can join us.

Join the fun

This year we'll take thousands of free-spirited

BEST OF GUIDES

Full color easy-to-scan format, focusing on Europe's most popular destinations and sights.

Best of England
Best of Europe
Best of France
Best of Germany
Best of Ireland
Best of Italy
Best of Spain

COMPREHENSIVE GUIDES

City, country, and regional guides with detailed coverage for a multi-week trip exploring the most iconic sights and venturing off the beaten track.

Amsterdam & the Netherlands
Barcelona
Belgium: Bruges, Brussels,
  Antwerp & Ghent
Berlin
Budapest
Croatia & Slovenia
Eastern Europe
England
Florence & Tuscany
France
Germany
Great Britain
Greece: Athens & the Peloponnese
Iceland
Ireland
Istanbul
Italy
London
Paris
Portugal
Prague & the Czech Republic
Provence & the French Riviera
Rome
Scandinavia
Scotland
Spain
Switzerland
Venice
Vienna, Salzburg & Tirol

HE BEST OF ROME

ne, Italy's capital, is studded with san remnants and floodlit-fountain res. From the Vatican to the Colos-, with crazy traffic in between, Rome nderful, huge, and exhausting. The ts, the heat, and the weighty history

of the Eternal City where Caesars walked can make tourists wilt. Recharge by taking siestas, gelato breaks, and after-dark walks, strolling from one atmospheric square to another in the refreshing evening air.

d *Pantheon*—which st dome until the ly 2,000 years old ry over 1,500).

of Athens in the Vat-fies the humanistic ce.

gladiators fought nother, entertaining ce.

Rome *ristorante*. ls at St. Peter's seriously.

Rick Steves guidebooks are published by Avalon Travel, an imprint of Perseus Books, a Hachette Book Group compan